Aloysius

Aloysius

By

Francis X. Levy

A Tribute To A Saintly Priest

Printed in the United States of America by RDS Printing and Graphics, 1714 Grevillea Court, Ontario, California 91761

Published in 2011 by Francis X. Levy
7124 Hellman Ave. Alta Loma, California 91701

For copies of this publication, contact
RDS Printing and Graphics 1714 Grevillea Court, Ontario, CA 91761.   (909) 923-8831

TABLE OF CONTENTS

To Father John F. Schweikert, M.S.C.

A True Hero Of The Lord

Acknowledgments

Continued support and assistance by my wife Mary was a vital and necessary contribution to the production of this book.

Timely participation and encouragement has been given through the years by Patricia Treece, a leading spiritual writer of our age.

Father Kevin Manion, Father Charles Carpenter, M.A.P. and Father Miguel Atucha, C.M.F. have made major literary contributions and are gratefully thanked.

Finally, a lasting tribute must be paid to the many devotees of Father Aloysius who have allowed their stories to be told by the interviews which are presented herein.

Cover design by Robert J. Saiz.

Psalm 63

O God, You are my God; I shall seek You tirelessly.
I long for You, I thirst for You, body and soul, as
parched and desert land without water. Such am I
as I gaze toward You in Your sanctuary, longing to
see Your power and Your glory.

For Your good pleasure is more precious than life.
My lips shall praise You. Thus will I bless You my
whole life long. In Your Name I will lift up my
hands in prayer. I shall be filled with happiness
and gladness; with joyful lips my mouth shall
praise You.

I shall be mindful of You as I lay me down to sleep.
Through the hours of the night I will remember
You. For You have become my helper. In the
shadow of Your wings I will rejoice. My soul clings
fast to You; Your Right Hand defends me.

Those who seek my life maliciously shall meet with
death. They shall be delivered to the sword; they
shall be the prey of wild beasts. But the king shall
rejoice in God. Everyone who worships Him shall
be victorious; but the mouths of those who speak
evil shall be stopped.

FOREWORD

The author of this book Francis Levy was one of Father Aloysius Ellacuria's spiritual sons. In the timeless -ness of God, he still is.

Their closeness was honed in good times and bad for each of them. Francis, for instance, met the Spanish Basque-born Claretian priest when Francis' beloved wife Marion was terminally ill with cancer. Although Marion received various remissions through Father Aloysius' prayers, she ultimately died, leaving a devastated, grief-stricken father to raise a young family of six grief-stricken children ages two to twelve. Far from turning against God or against the priest who could not save her life for all his self-giving, as many people have done in similar situations, Francis became ever closer to God and to his priest mentor, grateful to be one of Father's sons in God.

In a happier time, Father Aloysius was involved in the decision of Francis and his present wife of many years, Mary, to wed. The priest was already important in Mary Naughten's life - -she had gone on pilgrimage with Father, for one thing -- even before she met Francis.

Francis and Mary remained staunch friends of Father Aloysius until Father's death, even through some difficult times for their friend, when God permitted the genial Spaniard to be sorely tried by good people. For instance, in the Los Angeles church, men who felt his charismatic healing gift was gaining him too big a following saw that Father was quietly sent away from the diocese. (He was later permitted to return). In another trial, his Claretian Order permitted him to begin a new branch of the Order, then it was up to him to obtain sure footing for the foundation. Too, although he had the charism of healing for others and was himself once miraculously healed, there were the priest's own health problems as he aged. Through all these ups and downs of their lives, the Levy family and their priest mentor remained tied together by mutual prayer and love even when many miles separated them.

Francis came to believe Father Aloysius' virtues and extraordinary relationship with God should be known to the wider world beyond Father's large life circle. He wrote and self-published with his own money a book years before this one that testified to his spiritual mentor's effects on his own life. After that, in retirement Francis Levy devoted years to interviewing and videotaping those who knew Aloysius Ellacuria or had interacted with him in some significant way, such as having a dying family member healed. Out of this pure devotion, recently Francis has devoted immense amounts of time to the extremely laborious transcribing of those interview tapes on the late priest, in order to provide the documentation that is vital to promoting Father's Cause. Many of these make up a significant part of this second book.

The writer of this Foreword met Francis in the late 1980s during research for my book *The Sanctified Body* after my cloistered Carmelite friend Sister Veronica Doerner, O.C.D. told me about Father Aloysius' having been seen levitating by Los Angeles area Carmelites. I knew from years of researching saints and purported saints how saintly or otherwise an individual can look by judicious editing of a life! But in Francis Levy, a retired engineer, that is a member of a profession looking askance at the fanciful and devoted to getting details right, I had a treasure: a witness in whom one could have absolute confidence that he was "never carried away" when he spoke of even astounding things, such as Father Aloysius' gift of retaining the Eucharistic presence. It is to the quality of Francis' work assembling the details of Father's life, along with the testimonies of others (to whom Francis introduced me in many cases), that I came to believe Father Aloysius will be canonized one day. Francis identified irrefutably Father's heroic virtues as well as Father's complete submergence of his own will in God's, the two essentials of sanctity, plus Father Aloysius' utmost endeavor to form others in sanctity. Today I also know, from years of having Francis as a benefactor in my own work as well as a personal friend and mentor, that Francis' virtues are not, to put it in a way that won't raise the humble man's hackles, unworthy of his spiritual father. Another reason for absolute confidence in anything he says about Father Aloysius.

For all these reasons, I can think of no one better suited to report to you on a life that is intensely modern and very accessible, yet also has extraordinary mystical aspects. Francis named his earlier book on his relationship with Father Aloysius *Our Guide*. You will find in Francis Levy's biography of Father Aloysius a sure and trusted guide as well.

Patricia Treece

Father Aloysius as a Young Priest

PREFACE

What is it that would make one do significant research and write about a man unless he were very special and in fact most unusual. Certainly, such a man is the subject of this book. As these pages will relate, Father Aloysius Ellacuria, C.M.F. proved during his lifetime that he was special to such a degree as to be considered highly unusual. When Almighty God Himself selects one of His creatures upon whom to bestow certain unique gifts, this selection sets this person apart as one upon whom we are drawn to focus our attention . Then when the object of our gaze exhibits heroic virtue, he becomes a model for all and a provider of glory to his Creator.

It is the hope of those who have become acquainted with Father Aloysius either directly or indirectly, that he be raised to the Honors of the Altar. These hopes can only be realized through prayer and the diligent efforts of his petitioners. Nothing of course is meant to be unless it is the Will of Almighty God. Perhaps this book will be a means of uniting the faithful to solicit the granting of Sainthood by Our Heavenly Father upon our beloved Father Aloysius. When a Cause in his behalf is opened, this process will then be pursued. May God grant this favor to His people so that we may render Him Honor and Glory.

The natural boundary between France and Spain is well defined by the Pyrenees Mountains which extend about 270 miles. As you travel across these mountains from

Spain, moderate height and rolling farm land is the panorama. Nestled into this range on the Northern side is the French Basque Province and similarly on the South is the Province of the Spanish Basque where the largest city is Bilbao which dates back to the fourteenth century. Gothic architecture and the Guggenheim Museum are noteworthy symbols in this unique culture of Northern Spain.

Aloysius Ellacuria spoke little of his early life in the Basque city of Yurre where he had been baptized . But of significance was the fact that his Baptism took place on June 22, 1905, the day following his birth. In a family of nine children, Aloysius was the fourth child and the oldest boy.

Like many other works, this book in its present state has resulted from the expansion of the initial concept. Originally it was meant to be a brief account of a portion of the life of Father Aloysius in so much as it presented many elements of his interaction with me and my family. This approach was necessary in order to convey the main message: the sanctity of the man who was so blessed with special favors. Additionally, at the time of the first edition there was very little personal history available to draw upon. The result of this limitation was the production of two editions of "Our Guide," which for several years were the only books written about Father.

When the Second Edition of "Our Guide" was distributed, it fell into the hands of Father Javier Oroz, C.M.F. in Tolosa, Spain. He became so interested in this manuscript that he asked for permission to translate it into Spanish. Most willingly I granted his request and Fr. Oroz proceeded with the translation and publication of this work in Bilbao, Spain.

Some time thereafter in order to continue gathering information about Fr. Aloysius, I contacted Fr. Oroz in an attempt to get additional data. It didn't take Fr. Javier Oroz long before he spoke to Fr. Miguel Atucha, C.M.F. about my request. Very graciously, Fr. Miguel wrote in Spanish to Fr. Javier giving him extensive historical information. It was an exceedingly happy event to receive such a letter (handwritten by Fr. Miguel) which Fr. Javier forwarded to me. However, this letter was of little value for my purpose until Fr. Charles Carpenter, M.A.P. kindly provided a translation. This work by Fr. Charles is greatly appreciated.

Many people have aided me with this writing. It is readily seen herein that the in depth interviews which I was permitted to conduct could not have been done without full cooperation from the subjects. Their willingness to be questioned and to share their time and their hopes was absolutely essential. My wife Mary was always present to assist with this task. Additionally, during the writing of this book, she offered valuable counsel.

Father Kevin Manion was a most capable and constant advisor. I cannot measure the importance of having the personal secretary to Father Aloysius always available to call upon. He was a close friend and frequent visitor to our home even before his entry into the priesthood. It was at this time that he served as Father's secretary and chauffer. Thus it was he who brought Father to our relatively remote location for visits and relaxation.

During my college days, my English teachers worked hard to develop the necessary writing essentials for the science major that I was. In the last fifteen years it has been my good fortune to be an assistant to Patricia Treece who is a writer by schooling and profession. Her example and guidance were the ingredients that I needed so badly if I wished to assemble my work into a readable format.

It is my hope that this manuscript will give glory to Almighty God and reflect positively on those who shared their efforts with me. I give grateful thanks to all of them.

Whereas many of the events which are related herein are deemed to be miraculous or at least extraordinary, it must be emphatically stated by the author that he offers the following declaration:

In conformance with the decree of Pope Urban VIII, I submit the material in this publication for human consideration only. The Catholic Church unreservedly is the judge of extraordinary gifts of grace.

July 1, 2011
Francis X. Levy
Alta Loma, California

Chapter One

Father Miguel Atucha, C.M.F.

The use of Father Atucha's letter at the beginning of this book will serve to introduce the reader to the early religious life of Father Aloysius. The letter provides valuable details which would otherwise be difficult or impossible to obtain.

The following paragraphs constitute the entire text of Father Miguel Atucha's letter which he sent to Father Javier Oroz on my behalf:

Tolosa, Jan. 6, 1992
To Fr. Javier Oroz, C.M.F.

First of all, my fraternal greetings, together with my fervent wishes for your well-being and progress in holiness and the apostolate in this new year of 1992. And now you have the fulfillment of my commitment regarding the information on Fr. Juan Luis Ellacuria, C.M.F.

(1) Juan Luis de Ellacuria was born in Yurre (Vizcaya) in the neighborhood of San Cristobal, the product of a very Christian home. I have the impression that at that time there already a school in that neighborhood which was directed by a teacher from the diputation of Vizcaya, where the classes were given in Basque, our native language. I believe he always attended this elementary school. Consequently, we

1

practically didn't get to know each other until the very day of our entrance into the Minor Seminary of the Claretians in Balmaseda on Sunday July 30, 1916. After hearing Holy Mass very early at the Parish, we four candidates for the Claretian Seminary (Juan Luis Ellacuria, Crescencio Iruarrizaga, Juan Manzarraga, and the undersigned), accompanied by some relatives went together in the tranvia from Arratia to Bilbao. In Bilbao we took the train that goes to Balmaseda where we arrived at midday. I remember during recreation some of our new companions told us: "Tomorrow you can speak Basque, because it's the feast of St. Ignatius of Loyola."

(2) His entrance into the Minor Seminary. In those days, the atmosphere in our Minor Seminaries was of total separation from the world. We lived totally dedicated to a life of fervor, study and of formation aimed at our future religious life. It was something like trying to copy the life of the Child Jesus in Nazareth, of whom the Evangelist, St. Luke refers: "The Child grew and became stronger, filled with Wisdom; and upon the good pleasure of God remained." And, "Jesus progressed, according to His age, in wisdom and grace before God and men."

When we entered the above mentioned Claretian Minor Seminary, it was a day of leave takings; the first referred to those who were leaving to go and start their Novitiate in Segovia. And the second referred to the one who was the formator up to that time of the Minor Seminary, Fr. Juan Antonio Uriarte, who was leaving for his new assignment. And these leave takings were ending, and the greetings were being given to the new director of the Minor Seminary, Fr. Salvador Esteban, with whom we would live during the next four years, which was the amount of time it took for the formation of boys aspiring to religious life in our institute.

During those four years, I always saw Juan Luis dedicated to a life that was normal in every aspect. What stood out in him were his simplicity, his piety, his kindness and dedication to study. I believe he knew how to fulfill well the role of a hidden and fragrant violet. Regarding his studies, he was outstanding for his special aptitude for languages and for writing.

(3) His year of Novitiate. At the beginning of August, 1920, we left for Salvatierra of Alaba to begin the new novitiate year of the religious Province that extended from Segovia. We took the religious habit on the 14th of August; the Most Rev. Fr. Martin Alsina being Superior General of our religious Institute at that time. Since the building had to be adapted to the needs of a Novitiate, it turned out to be a year of many discomfits on the material level. Of course, this did not adversely affect Juan Luis at all. Since there was no field for games, in order to warm up or do some physical exercise during the recreation period, the only thing they could do was walk around, help with construction work, or play "four corners," and thus all of us were happy and satisfied.

Our Master of Novices was Fr. Antonio Fernandez, who satisfactorily fulfilled his task as representative of the Congregation. If Juan Luis had dedicated himself to digging solid human and Christian foundations during the Minor Seminary or in the Postulancy, he took real good advantage of his Novitiate year to empty himself completely into the perfect mold of his missionary vocation. I believe the Novitiate year was for him a year of extraordinary grace and unforgettable in that he carried it with him invariably for the rest of his religious life. Undoubtedly he was aspiring day by day toward the luminous date of his total consecration to the special service of God and the Immaculate Heart of Mary by the profession of his religious vows and his oath of permanence in the Congregation. That glorious day arrived on August 15, 1921, when , he professed for the first time, and for one year his sacred commitment. How joyful and happy Juan Luis looked on that much awaited day of his first Profession! How much he would have wished those vows, that oath and that sacred consecration had been perpetual….in order to repeat all during his lifetime: "Quod dixi, dixi"… "quod promissi, promissi"… "Placeat mihi quod dixi, et promissi"…

On the same afternoon of our first profession (in order to make room for the new novices) we took the train in Salvatierra to arrive at midnight in Beire (Navarra), where the Faculty of Theology was then located.

(4)   Juan Luis during his three years of Philosophy in Beire. A little before making his first profession, he had reached 16 years of age. In the prime of his first youth, he began his human and Christian perfection and the most faithful exercise of his new commitment as a soul consecrated to God with vow and oath. Juan Luis spent these three years of Philosophy, externally without hardly being noticed as a hidden and fragrant violet. His tenacious work was interior in his life of formation for his full and future missionary and cordimarian life . He was definitely convinced that no one can give what he doesn't have. And that the first and

most difficult conquest is that of oneself for God. We can resume these three years of his life of religious formation in these words: Juan Luis in the ordinary run of his daily life appeared extraordinary by his constant faithfulness to all his commitments. His Father Prefect of formation in those three years was Fr. Luis Maria Bravo, a man of deep convictions.

(5) In August of 1924 Juan Luis, together with his classmates, went from Beire to Santo Domingo de la Calzada (La Rioja) in order to take his first three years of Theology. At his 19 years of age, with great abundance of knowledge in different areas and with the constant practice of the virtues, Juan Luis started his theological studies that raised him higher and higher in divine and supernatural knowledge. He saw how one finds before him infinite treasures that are immense in their divine relationships. He saw how all his abundance in these subjects was as nothing in order to faithfully fulfill his mission as a cordimarian and Claretian apostle in the footsteps of Jesus Christ and of St. Anthony Mary Claret. It was evident that Juan Luis did not feel immediately inspired to external apostolate. Rather, he dedicated himself solely to interior prayer, sacrifices and good example. He remembered well what St. Francis Xavier had one day written to some Jesuit seminarians in Rome who were so desirous of going as soon as possible to the missions in the Indies: "For now your mission is there in Rome --- the mission of your adequate formation in order that later on you may be true apostles of Christ." The innocence and candidness of Juan Luis was almost proverbial among his companions. In this Our Lord was awaiting him with the first outward trial in order to begin to open his eyes to the daily reality of men. I don' t know

why, but one fine day I heard that Juan Luis was there in the recreations "discovering the roots" of the Basque words. Actually the Basque language has only between 300 and 400 "basic roots." It seems that some of his classmates were celebrating him for such an enterprise. But, oh human fallacy!

It was the third year of Theology. The reception of the fourth minor Order was getting closer (the Order of Acolyte). And on the list of the ones approved for this the name of Juan Luis did not appear! For him this amounted to a great disappointment. But I never heard him complain about it. Our Prefect of formation during these three years was Fr. Juan Maria Goricho, formator of the theologians for many years and with great success.

(6) And the final stage of Juan Luis ecclesiastical studies arrived. In August of 1927, from Sto. Domingo de la Calzada we went to the city of Segovia, where at that time the religious Province of Castille had its two years of moral theology, Canon Law, etc. For the first of these two years his Prefect of formation was Fr. Rufin de Guerica; and in the second year it was Fr. Ildefonso Martinez. Both of them were competent in the course work. Juan Luis took good advantage of these two years to complete his human, Christian, religious, priestly and missionary formation. Besides assimilating well the subjects proper to those two years, Juan Luis was increasing more and more his knowledge of the different ecclesiastical and religious subjects in the degree to which he approached his priestly ordination. But he could not be ordained with his classmates because he had not reached the canonical age.

(7) Year of Ministerial Preparation. In the month of August, 1929, the graduating class of new priests of the Provinces of Catalonia and Betica were united to start our so-called year of Ministerial Preparation for the Apostolate, in the town of Aranda de Duero (Burgos). Above all, we should sketch here the priestly ordination of Juan Luis de Ellacuria in the city of Burgos, at the hands of the Archbishop of the City on the 3rd of November, 1929. Finally so many and such aspired for wishes of his during his childhood and youth were to be fulfilled: To become another Christ in order to extend the reign of Christ over the whole earth!

The Father Prefect of formation during this year was Salvador Espina, very experienced in his years in this special assignment. Juan Luis, as always, dedicated himself in body and soul to this theoretical and practical preparation in the different priestly and missionary ministries. And as it would seem, he still had not completed the second part of the teaching of Jesus Christ to his Apostles: "Be as simple as doves but as prudent as serpents." I believe God permitted for him another trial (this time little), for his future experience. The superiors put Juan Luis and another of the young Fathers in charge of teaching Latin and French, respectively, to a young man of Aranda. Some time later, Juan Luis, with some bitterness on account of the disloyalty of his companion, gave me the following confidence: "It seems my companion only tried to win for himself the affection and good will of the young man commended to our respective classes." In fact, years later the other young Father left the Congregation.

Toward the beginning of the summer of 1930, the year of Ministerial Preparation was finished and the moment arrived for our respective assignments. Father

Juan Luis was assigned to our religious Province of the U.S.A. He left by ship from Barcelona and upon his arrival in Colon, on October 9, 1930, he wrote to our "Peers of the Congregation:" "On the 14th of this month I will be leaving from Colon for New York." And he finishes his missive with the following words: "We implore our brothers of the Congregation some prayers so that God Our Lord and the Heart of His divine Mother may straighten our path to the purest and most perfect attainment of the threefold aim of our beloved Congregation by the threefold sacrifice, which, because we are looking to the heights, we have just made with the greatest joy: the sacrifice of our family, of our language and of our country."

(8) And before ending my narration of my impressions of the childhood and seminary years with Juan Luis Ellacuria, I am going to point out two things: the first, his love for his native language, Basque. In spite of all, he accepted his assignment to the United States with joy, because that was where religious obedience was taking him. I used Juan Luis' services for the inscription on the prayer card in Basque I made for my priestly ordination. The second refers to a letter of condolence that Fr. Juan Luis sent to me from the United States on the occasion of the death of my brother, Juan Atucha, C.M.F., who was also a Claretian priest. This letter of condolence seems to me a perfect reflection of the soul of Father Juan Luis: all goodness... delicateness... religious brotherliness... an authentic spirit of holiness... May God raise up in all places many and holy priests and religious who are imitators of him... And may God bless his religious foundation abundantly. And if it is for His greater glory, may God make the words of

His Divine Son again come true: "He who humbles himself shall be exhalted;" in favor of Juan Luis de Ellacuria Echevarria. Amen.

Miguel Atucha, C.M.F.

Father Miguel Athucha, C.M.F

Chapter Two

<u>The Road To Sainthood</u>

As I read this letter by Father's classmate, I have to reflect in my own mind those qualities which I witnessed in Fr. Aloysius' life. I bear testimony to the fact that Father exhibited in his every day life those teachings which were imparted to him in the seminary. Father Aloysius was a man who lived in the company of the Lord. Every aspect of his being portrayed his total absorption in the Spiritual Life. Whenever he recited the Holy Rosary, he intently participated in the very Mysteries themselves. He never tired when it was time for prayer. Whenever someone came to him with a sickness, his compassion was so great that he appeared to have contracted the pain himself.

It is not unusual in the lives of the saints for them to experience a banishment from their diocese to some distant land. It seems that in the master plan which Our Blessed Lord has in store for his future saints, there comes the time for them to undergo this unique penance. This was surely the case for Fr. Aloysius when he was sent away to Phoenix, then San Antonio and finally to Spain. While this was mystifying to all of his followers, it presented yet another opportunity for Fr. Aloysius to excel in the virtue of holy obedience. Still, for those who loved him, his presence was deeply missed.

On July 17, 1995 while my wife and I were in Tecate, Mexico I asked Bishop Arzube what we could say in a book about Father Aloysius regarding his expulsion from the diocese years ago. He told me that we could say the following: "Religious authorities felt that he was drawing too many people and it was becoming a cult. For the good of the Church they felt that he should be transferred until things quieted down. Later on, he was allowed to return and Bishop Arzube made him one of his Chaplains for his episcopate ordination ceremony." It was in this manner that public acceptance was given back to Father Aloysius. Recent developments have pointed toward a gathering interest in the advancement of the "Cause" for this holy man. This process involves painstaking investigations into all elements of the life in question.

In the last twenty-five years there has been a significant accumulation of documentation on behalf of this project. An important factor however to be considered is that any miracles that may have occurred during one's lifetime cannot be attributable to an individual so as to satisfy the necessary Beatification requirement. Only those heavenly favors which occur after ones death can then be certified and regarded in this light.

For about ten years, my wife Mary and I traveled throughout Southern California, Arizona and Texas seeking out and interviewing people who had been in contact with Father Aloysius for various reasons. These interviews were recorded on video tape for preservation and as a means of obtaining the most effective documentation. At a later date, all of these interviews were further processed to the DVD format for more durability. There were at least fifty interviews and of this total, only some of them so far have been transcribed into computer format. It is this latter final process that allows such information to be presented for the reader. Thus, a significant section of this book will deal with these interviews. It is hoped that this method of presentation will acquaint the reader more intimately with Father.

Chapter Three

Fidel, Milagros, and Lupita Jimenez

On November 25, 1990, in their home in Alta Loma, California the Jimenez family greeted us on an early Sunday afternoon. We spoke at length first to Fidel who was born in the beautiful city of Leon Guanajuato in central Mexico on the twenty fifth of March 1947. Fidel, whose name means Faith, was raised in the city of Guadalajara, the capital of Jalisco. When he was nearing eighteen years of age, he journeyed to California with his mother and younger brothers. There they joined his father and older brothers to establish a permanent home for the family.

Fidel knew that it was not by chance that he met Milagros; he attributes this blessing to Our Lady of Guadalupe, for it was in this Church in El Monte that he met and later married Milagros who had emigrated from Cuba. Ultimately all of their children were baptized at Our Lady of Guadalupe Church.

Father Michael Nicolas, a Spanish priest was the one who first spoke of Father Aloysius to Fidel. There was no reason to be impressed by this priest whom he had never met but he felt that the meeting would occur some day. Fidel said that God told him the Blessed Mother was the one who was preparing the meeting at a time when there would be a real need.

Taking the older children, Fidel and Milagros went to Mexico City and Puebla for a vacation in 1979 leaving

Lupita and Jose with Milagros' mother because they were fearful of possible contaminated water (Monte-zuma's Revenge).

While staying with one of the aunts, at about eight at night Milagros began to cry saying: "Lupita--- there's something wrong with Lupita---let's go back." What do you mean, let's go back?" was Fidel's response. Milagros had the haunting feeling that something was happening to Lupita. This strange situation prompted Fidel to recall a recent event that had occurred in his life. It was a time of spiritual rejuvenation for him as he attended a Retreat. Many of the men who were with him on the Retreat were crying and thanking God for such tremendous spiritual gifts; their elation was profuse. Since he did not share in this jubilation, Fidel made three separate pleas on his knees before the Blessed Sacrament: "Lord, well You know what you are going to give me." After this brief statement, Fidel felt that the Lord didn't answer his request but instead replied: "I'm not going to give you anything." "What are You going to give me?" repeated Fidel. So, the next day, the fourth day of the Cursillo, Fidel returned to the Blessed Sacrament and asked again: "Lord, You know I'm so sad, how come You don't give me happiness?" Not hearing a verbal response but feeling that he got the same answer as before: "I'm not going to give you anything." Fidel was dismayed. After a similar entreaty on the following day, the answer that he received was the same as before. The continued repetition of this answer by the Lord was so strange to Fidel that he could only respond: "What do You want?" He sensed then that the Lord was asking him: "What are you going to give me?"

When he came out of the Retreat, Milagros was expecting Fidel to be so happy but he felt so sad. He told her: "It was very strange, Our Lord asked me what was I going to give Him. At first I said: I don't know; what do You want--- money? I'll double what I give."

The next day, after Milagros' plea to return home because of the impending peril for Lupita that she felt, they returned to the house of a relative in Mexico City and it happened that a little boy came running. One of Fidel's relatives then chided him: "How come you let the little boy run in the middle of downtown Mexico City with all of the terrible traffic?" The only boy that Fidel knew was his youngest son that had accompanied him on the trip. Since he felt that they didn't pay due respect to traffic laws in Mexico, Fidel was quite concerned with this episode and couldn't feel comfortable until he verified that it was not his son who had dashed out into the city. Fidel was now fully aware of the situation: "When something happens in his family, a little boy always comes. Someone else sees him or my wife sees him."

Once again, Milagros pleaded: "Let's go back, let's go back." But Fidel felt like St. Thomas, obviously doubting any urgent need. They continued their vacation and event.ually returned home via Alamos, Mexico to see Father Carlos.

When they got home, Fidel's mother-in-law was very upset because Lupita was so sick that they had taken her to the doctor. They hadn't called to relate this news in order not to upset them on vacation. Lupita was becoming anemic and was receiving iron and vitamins.

Then there was diarrhea and vomiting which prompted a virus diagnosis. Subsequent treatments proved to be useless and the girl gradually became worse. Her blood count dropped below seven. The doctor decided to go to the laboratory and do the blood test himself. When the doctor returned with a "very bad face," he let Milagros know that he had to put Lupita into the hospital. Milagros queried: "Is something wrong? Really bad?" But the doctor gave no response. Then Milagros added: "She looks very yellow, she doesn't scream, she doesn't eat she doesn't drink. Is it cancer? Is it her liver?" The only response that the doctor could give was to state that he didn't want to say anything until he had done further testing at White Memorial Hospital.

The diagnosis finally came—cancer in the blood, and they called it leukemia. At this time, the doctor felt great emotion because Lupita was only two years and five months old and it was necessary to transfer her to Children's Hospital. There she received the attention of eight doctors, the principal one being Doctor Higgins a woman. The unanimous conclusion they reached was acute lymphatic leukemia with a possibility of living another two years.

Hope for survival was now placed in the administration of chemotherapy. This was very difficult for Lupita and surely quite disturbing for Fidel; yet Milagros, who wasn't a very devout Catholic at that time, took it with tremendous faith. Fidel looked upon this sickness in his daughter as serving a beautiful purpose. And by it he came to realize that his wife was very strong.

On one occasion during the course of the chemotherapy treatments, while Lupita was being treated for the flu, the hospital staff had quite a bit of difficulty locating a vein for an immediate transfusion. When a vein couldn't be found in the arms, they went to the legs. When Lupita then began to say in Spanish: "I want my Papa," it made Fidel think back to the time of his retreat. He recalled Our Lord saying to him: What are you going to give me?" Then he thought: "O my God, this is what you were asking me when I went to the retreat, you're asking me for the life of my daughter." Soon after, the doctor returned and gave Lupita the transfusion.

Time flew by so that it was soon the twelfth of October and while Fidel was at work he received a call from Milagros saying that Lupita was dying---"She was in her crib with her eyes closed and she was as white as snow. There was no hope, she was ready to die." Already having been placed in a separate room, Milagros figured that this meant they were waiting for death.

Lupita's stomach had become enlarged and respiration was noisy. She repeatedly called for her Mommy to hold her. Then she would say: "Put me in bed, Mommy; oh, oh it hurt me." When she was again placed in bed, her breathing became labored. Instead of calling the doctor, Milagros went to the phone to call her husband. She told Fidel: "Remember that priest they told you about?" "Yes," he said. "Well, will you please go out and find him. Wherever he is, find him; she's dying." At that moment she felt like she had lost confidence in everybody. She decided that the best thing for her was to try to contact Father Aloysius herself since she had the phone number. When she phoned, she learned from the secretary that Father himself had returned from the hospital on the previous day---he was very sick; only half of his heart was functioning.

As Milagros began to cry, she explained to the secretary that her daughter was dying of cancer and she had heard from other people that Father Aloysius could "do a miracle." "I need to talk to him." When the secretary explained that it is actually Our Lord who performs miracles through him, Milagros quickly agreed that is what she meant. "Can you please do something?" Milagros asked. "Yes," was the reply. "I'm going to talk to him—it's not allowed but I'm going to talk to him."

Previously, Milagros never had a special devotion to the Blessed Mother but now, falling to her knees she spoke to Our Lady, reminding her of her anguish when she saw her Son on the cross. "I'm not worthy, but if you can, you can help me." Her entreaty to Our Lady was for a miracle and then she decided to leave it in the hands of the Blessed Mother.

After he had received the phone call from Milagros, Fidel went to Our Lady of Guadalupe Church to kneel in front of the Blessed Sacrament. He proceeded to pray: "O.K., my daughter's dying and You're the boss; who can be against You; who can oppose Your Will? But if You want to, You can help. You can save my daughter if it is Your Will." He then added: "Well yes, give me the strength if she dies."

Then Fidel went to the altar of Our Lady of Guadalupe. As he knelt there, he said the following prayer: "Oh Mama, you are the most beautiful Mother. You have been my Mother all my life. I love you more than my own mother. I trust you with everything I have . She cannot tell you at this time, but my daughter is dying and if you pray for her she can be cured; please help me."

With some difficulty, Fidel was able to find the Claretian Provincial House on Westchester Place in Los Angeles where Father Aloysius resided. When he knocked at the door, the secretary who was a nice lady asked what could she do. "Can I speak with Father Aloysius?" Fidel inquired. "No, you can't." she responded. "Why?" asked Fidel. "Oh, he just came out of the hospital and the doctor ordered that he have no visitors, no problems. He has to rest, half of his heart is paralyzed[1]. He has so many problems, so many diseases. He needs to rest and relax. He's dying himself; he's very sick." "Oh I'm sorry, very sorry; it's just that my daughter is dying." Fidel said. When the secretary could do nothing but sympathize with Fidel, he turned to leave but instead came back and looking at the woman, he told her: "Well, listen, what do you want me to tell my wife when I go back to the hospital and if my daughter is dead? And what do you want me to tell her. I came over here to talk to Father Aloysius and you'd said I couldn't see him, and this is our last chance." And she said: "O.K. come in."

After being invited to come in, Fidel waited for about forty-five minutes in the hall when he caught sight of an old man, bulky and heavy set; he was bald with big blue eyes---"The most restful eyes I've ever seen. He makes you feel like you want to kneel and confess your sins. He had a tremendous presence of authority. He came

---

[1] In all probability, this was a dysfunction of the heart chambers.

20

dragging his feet; he could hardly walk—he could hardly speak." "Are you Mister Jimenez?" Father said. When Fidel looked at him, his immediate thought was: "Oh my God, this man is dying." "I'm sorry Father, to bother you." "That's fine, that's fine, my son." Father replied.

Father looked at Fidel with so much mercy, so much kindness that he looked like Fidel's father or grandfather. Fidel felt truly sorry to bother him. "But I cannot go with you. How is Lupita?" Father said. "She's dying, Father." Fidel answered. Father said: "Well, I wish I could go but they won't let me go. I'm sick—half my heart is paralyzed." It was quite obvious to Fidel that Father was critically ill; he could barely breathe. Fidel was fearful that Father was going to die while he was standing right there by his side. He felt that he had better leave and let Father go to bed. He proceeded to explain to Father how sorry he was but that people had told him that God listens to him so he had come to ask him to pray for his daughter. When Father reminded him that he could not accompany him, Fidel said: "That's O.K., you can pray for my daughter from here and if God listens to you, it makes no difference where you pray. You can pray from the kitchen and from the bathroom or from the chapel. Wherever you pray, if God listens to you it's the same." "You believe that?" Father asked. "Yeah Father." Fidel answered, as he knelt down and asked for his Blessing. Using the standard Latin form for the Blessing, Father prayed: "Benedictio Dei Omnipotentis: Patris, et Filii, et Spiritus Sancti, descendat super te et maneat semper. Amen." Father would not let Fidel stand but instead told him that he was going to give him another Blessing for Lupita. Thus, he gave a second Blessing as he looked toward the hospital. When Fidel stood, Father

21

accompanied him to the door. As they were walking, Fidel said: "One thing I ask, if my daughter dies that I should not curse God for the death of my daughter." "No, no, no, we're going to pray for her health. Go in peace;" was Father's comforting response.

Concurrently, in the hospital, after crying and praying for about a half hour, asking Father Aloysius to help her, "something came over her" and Milagros began to feel very happy. She screamed: "Oh, thank God, he hears me; he's praying for my daughter." At that moment, Lupita awoke and sat up in the crib. "Mommy, what am I doing here? I want to eat. I want to drink. I want to play." That was the very moment Fidel had talked to Father Aloysius on October 12th, the feast of Our Lady of Pilar.

When Fidel arrived at the hospital, both mother and daughter were asleep. When she awoke, Milagros joyfully announced the spontaneous recovery of Lupita.

The next day when they went to bring flowers and give thanks to Father Aloysius, he told them: "No, no, no, no, don't thank me. It was the Blessed Virgin Mary who had asked for the healing of your daughter."

Then on Saturday, Father was able to leave the Provincial House and go by station wagon with Fidel to the hospital. There he proceeded through the wards blessing many of the children as he walked. Fidel exclaimed that Father knew who was going to live and who was going to die---he knew the state of the souls. Suprisingly to a doubtful Milagros, even the father of a Jewish baby allowed his child to be blessed. At this point, Father turned to Milagros and smiled.

Once again, we discussed the time following Lupita's cure. Several visits were made to the hospital where the staff was trying to convince Fidel and Milagros how important it was for them to continue with the chemotherapy. Because Milagros was adamant in her refusal, the attending intern sought out Dr. Higgings, the head of the cancer department in Children's Hospital. She too was not successful in her pleas to Milagros. As the days went by, the hospital personnel attempted to convince Fidel and Milagros of the great danger they were being exposed to by stopping the medicine. Dr. Higgins stated that Lupita would be dying in three to six months. Surely enough, in six months, she died. Who died, Lupita? No! Dr. Higgins died. This young doctor had died as a result of an accident. When she was returning from her vacation, someone ran a red light.

During this entire interview with Fidel and Milagros, Lupita sat silently. So I asked her age. "Thirteen," Lupita responded. "Thirteen?" I repeated. "How do you feel Lupe? You don't feel sick? You don't look sick. Do you feel sick?" "No," she was quick to answer.

At the present time, Lupita who is thirty two years of age is a Sister with the Trinitarians of Mary at Mount Tabor in Tecate, Mexico and Francis and Mary have seen her on numerous occasions. She looks and acts perfectly healthy.

Chapter Four

June Johnson

On October 10, 1992, there was a gathering in Torrance, California at the home of Mrs. Pat Arneson. A group of people had come there after the Mass at St. James Church in Redondo Beach. The celebrant of this Mass had been Father Gregory Hanks, M.A.P., a long time friend of ours, one of the early members of the congregation founded by Fr. Aloysius. Many of the people at this gathering were new faces to me, particularly a young lady named June Johnson. When I learned that she had a story she would like to tell, I immediately assembled my video equipment and proceeded to conduct an interview.

June Johnson who lived in Ventura, California had always been a native of Ventura County but had spent her years in various cities. At the age of thirteen she moved from Moorpark to Oxnard where she remained for twenty-eight years, the present time of this interview. June had lost her husband five years earlier.

In 1970, June's sister Gloria Stott told her about a priest who had healing powers. The priest was to be coming to a certain house in the city of Thousand Oaks, California. The opportunity to meet this priest appealed to June because of the concern she had for her son, Richard, a very bad asthmatic. Various medications had proven to be ineffective in the treatment of Richard; maybe this priest could do something. Nevertheless, the thought of any success with this approach was somewhat foreign to June. She knew that such things do happen, but she was reluctant at times to believe it.

"Why don't you go see Father Aloysius?" Gloria told June. In spite of her reluctance, June said: "O.K., I'll go." At this first meeting with Father, June was not impressed. However, when it came time for her to leave, Father gave her a Blessing. "I will not explain why---I cannot explain why---but I had a feeling inside I had never experienced before and I have not experienced since. It was an internal feeling and this is the God's truth---I was so happy, I cried from Thousand Oaks all the way home to Ventura." She said.

In their conversation, Father had told June to bring her son down to Los Angeles to a Guild meeting there for five consecutive First Saturdays. June's husband who was not Catholic didn't believe in this situation but he did agree to go along with it. So, Richard was brought to the Guild meeting at the Claretian Provincial House as directed. The boy became very tired and fell asleep in the back of the station wagon as they were leaving Los Angeles. Not only did he sleep all the way home, but continued to do so after he was put in his own bed.

Sudden drowsiness by Richard, now occurring every First Saturday, was very strange to June who had two girls who were "bouncing all over the place." She was puzzled as to the reason Richard would sleep all the way home.

Aloysius

Richard was ten years old when he first met Father in the early seventies. Through the Blessings of Father Aloysius, the asthma disappeared and has not returned.

After I queried her, June could not relate any other unique experiences when she was with Father. I was curious about her husband who was not a Catholic. She said: "My husband was not Catholic. He was not baptized. When he died, we had been married for 28 years and he died five years ago this past June." On one occasion, Father Aloysius came to bless the Johnson residence. When Father had gone out into the garage to complete his blessing, June told me: "My husband acted funny because Father was there. I apologized and I told Father--you know, Father, Richard is not Catholic and I'm very worried about him. He's not even baptized. And he told me: 'June, don't worry; when he dies, he will die a Catholic.'" And it came to pass, that just as Father Aloysius had said, six months before he died, he received his baptism.

To satisfy my interest, I asked June if she had any other association with Father---did she bring other people to him. "Oh, yes, yes." She replied. "There were so many people that wanted to see him. When he was over at the house, we had a house full of people. And like I say, he didn't impress me but there was something about this man that was overpowering---overwhelming, I can't explain. "

These comments prompt me to wonder how many other people were influenced by Father Aloysius.

June continued to relate her experiences: "All of our married life I dreamed of the day that my husband and I would receive Communion together. When the day came that we had to take my husband to the hospital, it was Father's day. I called Monsignor Beeterman, the priest at Sacred Heart Church. He came immediately to the hospital to give my husband the Last Rites. It was beautiful because my husband could not take the whole Host, and Monsignor Beeterman----I can't tell you without crying----" At this point, I interjected: "That's all right. That's fine. Take your time." After a pause, June continued: "Monsignor Beeterman took the whole Host and broke it in half and gave my husband half and gave me half. Thank you God." "How long after that did he die?" I asked. "He died at 1:20 the next morning." She said. "It was beautiful---it was something I always dreamed of. God permitted it." His funeral was at Sacred Heart Church in Ventura.

Father Aloysius

Chapter Five

Gloria Stott

On the same morning that I spoke to June Johnson, I had the opportunity to interview her sister Gloria Stott, who was the one to speak initially of Father Aloysius. Margaret, a dear friend and the wife of one of Gloria's cousins knew Father and was the impetus for Gloria's attendance at the regular First Saturday Guild in Los Angeles. This was during the late sixties.

Gloria invited Father to bless her house. She had no special need of her own, but by having Father come to her house it provided a means for others to meet and pray with him. However, Gloria had a lot of boys in her family and she felt that they were not faithful to the Church. Upon learning this, Father said that he would pray for them all the time.

Gloria spoke of the numerous gatherings at her house and at her sister's house when Father Aloysius was present. She also recalled one Mass that she had attended: at the elevation, when Father raised the chalice: "His voice struck a note that brought a tear to everyone in the church, including my sons. The Altar Boys looked up at Father Aloysius because the tears were running down their faces---all our faces---everybody. They weren't crying, it's just that tears were running down. The Holy Spirit came to all of us there at the time."

Gloria spoke of the picture she had taken of Father three weeks before his death and she also recalled the special indulgences he had placed on her religious articles. She had forgotten the significance of the A B C D blessings she received so I reminded her that they stood for Apostolic, Brigantine, Crozier and Dominican special indulgences. June then showed her own elation when she remembered that Father had given her daughter Lisa First Communion, after he received permission to do so from Sacred Heart Church. The more we spoke, the easier it was for old memories to be awakened. Gloria talked about her large family of boys and the final addition of the tenth child which was the only girl. She was so happy that she had visited Father upon his return from Fatima so that he could bless the child. After the blessing, Father told Gloria that the child was going to be a saint. What a tremendous encouragement this statement gave to a woman so steeped in her Faith.

Chapter Six

Francis A. Blackman

Francis A. Blackman was referred to me by Patricia Treece who is an esteemed Spititual writer in Portland, Oregon. With such a recommendation, I sought him out in West Covina, California on a rainy January 7, 1995. What an opportunity this was to converse with someone who lived with Father and the Claretians in the Los Angeles Provincial House on Westchester Place.

Francis, a native of San Gabriel, California was baptized at the San Gabriel Mission. While he was attending the San Gabriel Mission High School, he responded to the call for volunteer help with the Claretian Fathers at the Provincial House. It's a good thing that he offered his help because no one else spoke up. It was now in the early fifties and Francis was about sixteen years of age. Soon, one of the priests at the Mission took him to meet Fr. Aloysius. "Immediately, he gave me one of his profound Blessings and I felt so impressed with the presence of God and his awareness that I've never forgotten it." This was Francis' expression. This experience added momentum to an interest in religious life that had been present for many years in his youth. As time went on at school, Francis made known his desire to return to the Provincial House. Thus it was that he was able once again to see Fr. Aloysius. He took advantage of this opportunity to tell Father that he was interested in becoming a Brother. His wishes were granted, and the Claretians gained a new member.

At the Provincial House, Fr. Aloysius was the Novice Master for a couple of years. Although only one year in the Novitiate was required, Francis actually spent about three years there because he began his work as a Brother at the Provincialate. Then it was that he experienced the flood of visitors who came to seek help from Father. He himself was blessed with the special counseling that Father gave to the Novices and he was also able to attend Father's Masses and see firsthand this "highlight of Father's life---his Eucharistic love for Jesus in the Mass." "His Mass would last for over an hour and he would be so taken up with his Mass. There was one time in particular," Francis continued, "during one of his Masses, when he elevated the Host, he was so taken up, so absorbed in the presence of God that he was there for quite a while and then he motioned to me to come up to the altar." When Francis was at his side, Father said: "Where am I?" Francis believed that such a moment he was so privileged to witness was the ultimate experience of a Novice, the Eucharistic center of his life.

So many times Francis would see Father praying in the Chapel, "totally dedicated in the presence of God." Energetically, Francis continued: "And when he would give his talks, they were so imbued with the faith life. His faith was so strong; it was faith, faith, faith. And his whole life, the ultimate faith was love---love in action." In all of his ways, Francis could detect a constant prayerfulness, a deep relationship with God in his life, in his actions, in his prayers, in his thoughts and in his faith life. Francis felt so privileged to have such a powerful example in his life. As a Novice, Francis said that Father's door was always open to him. When Francis sought his counsel, Father would tell him just to continue the faith life.

Another aspect of Father Aloysius that Francis emphasized was dedication to the Blessed Mother. He let the Novices know that they were the Sons of Mary and the Sons of God. He instilled a deep devotion in his Novices for the Mother of God and taught them to pray the Rosary often.

When I questioned Francis as to whether he had ever seen anything externally extraordinary about Father, his response was certain that he never had. Aromas, or levitation were phenomena that he definitely did not witness. But he was quick to say that he was well aware that in Father's relationship with God there was an extraordinary divine presence.

After several years with Father Aloysius, Francis developed a very close relationship with him. For Francis it was very special. In fact, he remembers the time that Father defended him in front of everybody else with the words: "Well, maybe Francis was a little imprudent but none of you have the desire to be a saint like Francis."

Francis recalls the pain and suffering which Father Aloysius endured. A number of times upon retiring at night, Father told Francis that he had "real difficulty in breathing." Alarmed by the loud sounds which he heard, Francis would go over to Father's room asking: "Father, are you O.K.?" Apparently he was, although he was gasping for breath. Francis believed that some of Father's problem was due to the stress of his daily life. This was not only his analysis, one of his doctors had said that "he should try to relax a little more and do away with some of the stress." Of course, many people profited by the blessings and prayers of this holy priest. Francis was a witness to this.

Father Aloysius was very intent in acquainting the Novices with the Holy Constitution of the Claretians. By taking one chapter at a time, he would meticulously and conscientiously explain everything. At other times, Francis had the good fortune to drive Father to various other churches where he would celebrate Mass. In this way he attended many of Father's Masses -----and they were quite long.

Francis remembered the Guilds which Father inaugurated in honor of The Blessed Mother. He remembered Mrs. Shipstad, of the Shipstad and Johnson Ice Follies, as a Guild participant. He knew this staunch supporter very well.

After being a Claretian Brother for approximately twenty years, Francis Blackman was sent to an island near to Zamboanga, Mindanao in the Philippine Islands to do mission work from 1969 to 1972. Within that period he met a native Filipino woman named Nanita. She was a Moslem who converted to Catholicism. It is rather obvious that Francis played a major role in this conversion----he is her Godfather. Soon thereafter in 1975, Francis left the Claretians and married Nanita. This marriage required a special dispensation because of Francis being Nanita's Godfather.

Francis has a brother, Joseph who was a Claretian Brother for about twelve years serving as a cook. He also

Aloysius

has a sister, Sister Aloysius, who was a Carmelite nun for many years. She spent two years in Oklahoma and when she left the Carmelites she attended and graduated from San Diego University. Strangely enough, all three of the Blackman family who had been Religious, happened to get married on their thirty- ninth birthday.

Chapter Seven

<u>Ed and Frances Collins</u>

On April 25, 1996 in Phoenix, Arizona we interviewed Ed and Frances Collins at their home. Many years earlier, Frances' mother had met Father Aloysius through a friend from Cleveland. The friend had spoken so much about Father that it prompted Frances' mother to find him at Immaculate Heart of Mary Church in Phoenix. Soon thereafter, Ed and Frances also journeyed to the same Church to see Father. A second occasion for them to meet Father was in Fatima while on a tour.

During their tour, Ed and Frances were completely surprised to see Father celebrate Mass. They had not known that he was in the same chapel. With just two hours remaining for them to stay at this location, they anxiously sought to visit with Father after Mass. Frances said: "I did want to talk to Father but I saw him 'above the ground' so I didn't want to interrupt him; and I didn't want to lose him either in the crowd. So I was kind of skeptical about what I should do." Immediately, I spoke up and asked Frances: "When you say you saw him 'above the ground,' what do you mean by that?" She did not hesitate in replying: "He was not----his feet were not on the ground." "Was this during Mass?" I asked. "No," she said, "this was after Mass; after it was over and he was walking away." So I questioned further: "And he was in the air, you mean?" Again she answered: "Well, he was--- his feet did not touch the ground." At this point, I turned to Ed and asked: "How about you, Ed, did you see the same thing?" His response was different: "No, I didn't see the same thing. I was looking more or less---I just saw a glimpse--- there were so many people around there. I just saw a glimpse of his back and he was walking with another priest, I believe." I questioned again: "Had you seen this phenomena at all at any time during Mass or only after Mass?" Frances answered: "I didn't know he was-----after Mass because the way the Chapel was, it was packed." Ed added: "And it was small too." His wife continued: "And we were in the back and we didn't know who was saying the Mass." Again, Ed spoke: "We were back outside. There was nobody inside where he was saying the Mass; just another priest or his altar boys."

Ed and Frances had been referring to the old Chapel in Fatima so I asked my wife Mary, if she had been in that particular Chapel. Yes, she had been there but she could not identify what they were saying when they spoke of a separation for the celebrant of the Mass. The discussion centered on the new Chapel, a larger one that replaced the old one. Intent on pursuing creditability, I asked if he was actually walking above ground. Ed and Frances both agreed that it was when he was leaving, after Mass.

Again Frances reflected on her earlier statement about Father being "above ground" when she said: "And then he was just going away. So I didn't know whether I should interrupt him or---but I did want to see him. So then when I finally said, Father---I called his name, and then I saw that he was out of his ecstasy. That's the way I figured it." "He came down to ground then, huh"? I asked. She replied: "Then he came down to ground; yes." Not wanting to dismiss the matter without conviction, I asked: "About how long could you estimate you saw him in that condition above ground?" Frances replied: "Less than five minutes." "But it would be that long, huh?" I said. She pondered for a moment and then turning to her husband said: "Hmmmm, maybe about three; wouldn't it?" Ed re-enforced his former statement when he said: "Well, I don't know, I didn't see him."

I concluded that it was time for me to explain my position with these queries, so I did so, saying: "I ask these questions and I ask them in different ways. Perhaps it may sound boring to you, because people like good documentation if they ever use this for a story about Father. Maybe I won't think of all the questions, and if I try different approaches, I hope that somewhere along the line I'll hit the information that they are looking for." With an "O.K.", Frances Collins agreed with me. I continued: "So, was anybody with him when he was levitating?" She answered: "Yes, he had an aide with him and Father Charles mentioned his name but I don't remember it. He was, I would say in his fifties, a grey haired gentleman; handsome man, and he was with Father." "Were they conversing perhaps?" I asked. "That I didn't notice." She said. I continued with the question: "About how far away from him were you at this time?" "About four feet, hmm, ---yes, that's it," was her answer. I questioned further: "So, were you walking parallel to him or across his path?" She was definitive in her response, saying: "No, actually we were just standing there." Doggedly, I continued: "So he passed you then?" Patiently she stated: "He came out from the Chapel and we were on this other side. So then I saw him going away from us and that's when I wanted to call him," she said. At this point, I spoke: "Well, if you had an encounter of this sort for somewhat around five minutes-------" Frances Collins interjected: "Maybe not that long." I, then repeated her statement: "Maybe not that long." Her reply was: "Yeah, but like I said, I wanted to talk to him but I didn't want to interrupt. So, I was in a quandry." At this point in our discussion, both Ed and Frances agreed that to them it seemed as though Father was not totally concentrating on his present surroundings.

Mary asked when was the very last time they had seen Father. Ed didn't recall exactly but Frances thought it was in 1972. It was not an occasion for one of the Novenas nor was it for a Mass, it was a visit at Fr. Aloysius' invitation. Although Father had previously given some advice to a family member, no one accompanied Frances and Ed.

Neither Ed nor Frances had ever experienced any special aroma when in Father's presence during approximately six years that they had seen Father in Los Angeles. Both Ed and Frances were visibly impressed as they described the Blessings that Father used to give. They described these profound Blessings as they happened in both Los Angeles and at the Immaculate Heart of Mary Church in Phoenix.

We then chatted about several instances that had occurred at the residence on Westchester Place and spoke briefly about the various residents like Father Ambrosi and Kevin Manion. Then, once again our interview drifted back to Fatima where the Collins's had gone with no fore knowledge of Father Aloysius being there. Again, in search of concrete data, I asked: "Is there any way I can talk you out of seeing him levitate?"

The response given by Frances Collins was a terse: "I saw him." Not one to quit, I pursued the inquiry: "What makes you so certain that you saw him?" She wasted no time in repeating her claim: "I did see him. That's all I can say. I did see him." Then, Ed turned to his wife and said: "How high were his feet off the ground, do you know that?" Frances answered: "I'm very poor at heights----a couple of inches. Maybe three inches." I followed with: "Could you show me with your hands---about?" She then proceeded with a little demonstration. "He was higher than his aide. He was just up." I wanted to know if there could have been an obstruction like perhaps a wall that was in the way blocking their vision of the bottom of Father's feet. Frances said: "No, I saw him definitely, like I see you right there." Then I said: "And then when you called his name, that's when he came down?" Frances was firm in her answer: "That's when he came out of his ecstasy. That's the only way I can see it."

Then I took a different approach: "Can you describe his facial expression or condition at the time that he was levitating?" "No." was her brief reply. "Did it appear normal?" I asked. Steadfast in her conviction she said: "Yes, to me it did." At this point, I turned to Ed and asked if he had seen it. Ed couldn't confirm or deny the levitation because he wasn't actually looking at Father's feet at this time; he was looking straight ahead.

Mary brought up an interesting event then that she remembered from her previous pilgrimage with Father. She said that when she was in a church in a little Italian village, her roommate Katherine Morrow saw Father levitate when he was on the altar. Mary herself, however did not see this. We then began to discuss a previous interview that I had had with Katherine Morrow. I made it known that when I tried to get more details from Katherine it was rather late in her life and soon after she died. Therefore I wasn't able to get the details I wanted. Mary added surety to Katherine's experience when she spoke about how firm Katherine was.

Frances spoke of various conversations she had had with Father. It was obvious from her recollection that Father had stressed a point with her regarding the disposition of monetary gifts made to him. He was firm in his statement that money given to him would go either to the Claretians (his own order) if it was so directed, or to the order he had founded, if it was so directed in that manner. He stressed the fact that he would not give money to an improper source but rather that he would always honor the intensions of the donor.

Both Ed and Frances were greatly impressed by Father's sanctity which became most obvious in his manner of blessing---never rapid ---never fleeting. He always took his time and meditated as he prayed. Though the visits with Father made by Ed and Frances were not as numerous or lengthy as those made with others, it was quite obvious that Father Aloysius has a lasting remembrance with both of them.

Father Aloysius Blesses Religious Articles

Chapter Eight

Bishop Juan Arzube

On February 20, 1991, I had the privilege of interviewing Bishop Juan Arzube an Auxiliary Bishop to Archbishop (now Cardinal) Roger Mahony who is the head of the Los Angeles Archdiocese, the largest in the United States. This Archdiocese is divided into five Regions with Bishop Arzube in charge of the San Gabriel Pastoral Region. Bishop Arzube was a close friend of Father Aloysius and therefore an ideal subject for an interview. He was born in Guayaquil, Ecuador the son of a surgeon. He completed his high school and college education in Ecuador after living for a time in England. At a later date he attended Rensselaer Polytechnic Institute in Troy, New York and was granted a degree in Civil Engineering. As an engineer, he worked in Ecuador and then in 1944 moved to Los Angeles. In response to my request for some background information, Bishop Juan stated:

"I was born in Ecuador, South America and I was a late vocation . Before studying for the seminary, I was a Civil Engineer. I also dabbled in dramatics. I was the voice of actors in Hollywood. I was the voice of Peter Lorre, among others, in Spanish. Eventually as a result of a retreat, I went to the seminary. I studied for the priesthood and became a priest in 1954 and then was chosen to be a Bishop by Pope Paul VI in 1971. I knew Father Aloysius and admired him, a very spiritual man, he was my Spiritual Director for several years. When I was ordained a Bishop, I asked him to be my Chaplain. A Bishop to be, always has two priests with him as Chaplains right there on the altar on the day of ordination."

"I sent several people to him when I realized he had the power of healing. I noticed that when he had no power to cure the person, he would just say: 'Well, I will pray for you.' And whenever he would say you don't have to go to your doctor, then I realized that he knew that the person was taken care of."

"One such case was that of a lady from Ecuador who called me to say that she had made an appointment at St. Vincent's Hospital to have her cancerous tumor removed. This was on a Friday, I believe, and the appointment was for Monday. I told her about Father Aloysius and said: 'If you want, why don't you go see Father Aloysius and see what he would have to say.' Well, he Blessed her and told her that she did not need the operation but that if she felt better having it, she could, but that she could cancel the operation. So she did, with all faith in God and in him. The tumor never developed and she never had cancer again. She is always very grateful to Father Aloysius and has done many merciful works in his name in Ecuador."

Since the power of suggestion might sometime pose a doubt, the Bishop then spoke of a case of a youngster who was about six years old who had a bleeding nose. If you just touched his nose or if he was out in the sun too much, it would start to bleed. The mother had been taking the child to UCLA for treatment. When Bishop Arzube recommended that she take him to see Father Aloysius, she did so. Father Blessed him and told him he would be all right and that he didn't need any more medicine but that if he wanted to do so, he could take it. Later, the mother told the Bishop that the night that Father had Blessed him was the first night the child had been able to sleep for eight hours. Then when she took him to UCLA, they said the medicine must have been working marvels because he's so much better.

Another case which the Bishop recalled pertained to the wife of a doctor. Being a doctor, he had taken his wife to numerous specialists at the well known clinics. No one was able to take care of her illness. After being Blessed by Father Aloysius, she was cured to the utter amazement of the doctors.

The following text is copied from the Tidings arch-diocesan paper dated January 11, 2008:

"Retired Los Angeles Auxiliary Bishop Juan A. Arzube, among the country's first Hispanic bishops ordained in the post-Vatican II era, died Dec. 25 in Los Angeles. He was 89, and had lived at Nazareth House in West Los Angeles since 2002.

A funeral Mass was celebrated Dec. 31 at the Chapel of the Risen Christ at Holy Cross Cemetery in Culver City for Bishop Arzube, the second Hispanic bishop ordained in the U.S. (after Auxiliary Bishop Patrick Flores of San Antonio) when he was made a Los Angeles auxiliary in 1971. His involvement with various issues in the church and in the community prompted new outreach to Hispanics in the Los Angeles Archdiocese."

Chapter Nine

Father Mario Lopez, O.C.

It was in Phoenix, Arizona on January 26, 1991 when Mary and I were visiting Father Frank Ambrosi, C.M.F. that we heard about Father Mario Lopez and had the opportunity to interview him.

Father Mario, who was one of eight children , was born in Chicago in 1942. He was ordained a priest in 1976 a member of the Carmelites after having been a Brother for many years.

He first met Father Aloysius in 1973 because he was intrigued by a conversation he had had with a Dominican nun who had referred to Father as being a special priest. It so happened that a priest in the Monastery with Father Mario also knew Father Aloysius and offered to provide an introduction for him. It was through a mutual friend Maria Ross, that the meeting took place when she provided Father Mario with the address of the Claretian Provincial House. Specifically to go to confession, Father Mario went to this Claretian residence. After confession, Father Aloysius smiled and told Father Mario: "You will become my spiritual son; I will see you again." Father Mario didn't know what that meant to be a spiritual son but it felt very special and he wondered about a future meeting since no date or details had been set for one. Very definitely, several weeks later, the occasion arose and with this second opportunity, there began a relationship which lasted until Father Aloysius' death in 1981.

From this relationship, Father Mario carried a profound impression of the humility of Father Aloysius and of the great love which he shared. This love was exemplified by total selflessness in giving himself to others. It was not self deprecation but rather the action that resulted from someone who was filled with the Lord and allowed the Lord to shine through him. Father Mario describes the charity which he saw in this holy priest as a total and unconditional love that "just radiated from him." Because of this, he felt drawn to remain in his presence, always wanting to prolong the visits. These visits were always brief but after confession or a bit of conversation, there would always be a special Blessing which left Father Mario joyful and light-hearted. He relates that he had not noticed anything special physically about Father Aloysius until after one of his visits as he was approaching his car to return to the Monastery: "I noticed a strong odor of flowers; it struck me, and I looked around to see if anything was in bloom--if there were any flowers around. And there was nothing. I thought it strange and I wondered to myself whether that had come from him----so I presumed I smelled (it) myself; I didn't have any cologne on; or anything. And then I didn't think any more of it."

Through Spiritual Direction, Father Mario had been advised by Father Aloysius to live an active life as a Carmelite, whereas he refers to himself as being stubbornly resisting this advice in favor of the hermetical life instead. Father Aloysius would say: "No, your vocation is to live the active life. Live as a contemplative but live the active life." "And I kept insisting, no, and I want to do this other thing." So finally, Father Aloysius said: "Just a moment." "And he began to pray; he went into a very deep prayer." Father Mario continues. "It was-----I knew that he was no longer there present with me and I simply waited patiently. When he came back to himself, he said to me: 'The Blessed Virgin Mary said that you will live the hermetical life for a while.' And he couldn't tell me anything more. I knew that he had been in prayer and that either he heard a locution or he saw a vision; I don't know. But anyway it was just very natural."

Here again are Father Mario's words: "Different times he would tell me things that came to pass. The first time I remember that happening, I was going to make a retreat at a Trappist Monastery. I said I was going to go to this particular Monastery and he said: 'Can you give my greetings to Father Emmanuel'?----who is at another Monastery in Utah! And I thought to myself, well, I can't give greetings to that priest because I'm not going to see him." When the time came and Father Mario went to the particular Monastery as planned, it was not possible for him to make the retreat there at all. The only place that he could go was to the Monastery in Utah. So there he did see Father Emmanuel and gave him the greetings which Father Aloysius had requested.

Then again, Father Mario tried to describe the unique feeling which came to him while in the presence of Father Aloysius. "Just being in his presence, I didn't want to leave; there was something so special about him. I would think to myself several times how neat it would be if I could simply be around this priest and serve him in any capacity. So, I was delighted one time when he asked me to help him out by driving him some place. At the time I was not yet a priest; I was a Brother. He was very grateful and we chatted in the car. Another Claretian priest also came along. He invited me inside to the talk that was being given and I drove him back. But in that little time I came to see him in a different light; it was no longer in the Spiritual Directing setting. He was a very human, warm and open and kind individual that I had really always known him to be. The only other thing that I could relate is how (greatly) he affected individuals who came into his presence. My brother met him once only and since that time he has had a great devotion to Father Aloysius and prays for him constantly."

One other incident came to memory for Father Mario regarding a relative whom I will call Adam. Adam had been going with a girl for many years, had been living with her and wanted to get married. He asked Father Mario to marry him but Father felt uncomfortable (since) he hadn't been to church in many, many years. Adam had a fierce temper and was not conducive to the mentioning of church or any mention of having been to church; he would fly off the handle.

Father Mario spoke to Father Aloysius about the problem and sought his advice. The advice that he received was that we should pray for a miracle of grace. These were strange words to Father Mario, so they were further clarified with this instruction given by Father Aloysius: "Pray; we will pray and leave it in the Lord's hands. You go home and tell your relative to come to me to make a confession and then the marriage will go on". Father Mario left in trepidation not knowing how to approach this relative. What should he tell him? How could he tell him to go to this priest and go to confession? When he was able to gather up enough courage, Father Mario did as he was instructed when he said: "Adam, since you're going to get married and it's going to be in the Church, it would be proper that you make a good confession before you had the marriage and I know a priest who is very good who would hear your confession." To his absolute astonishment, Adam looked at Father Mario and gave a one word reply: "Fine." When the arrangements had been made, Adam was taken to the Provincial House. Confession took about twenty minutes and brought Adam out in tears. Father Aloysius then Blessed him and gave him a rosary for him and his future wife. Before he bestows these gifts, Father always Blesses them. This was probably the last time that Adam was to see Father Aloysius but with these brief encounters, Adam fell in love with him and continues to pray.

Father Mario remembers that it was Father Aloysius who encouraged him to become a priest and continued to correspond as his Spiritual Father until his death.

The final episode that Father Mario spoke of concerns a time in their early relationship when Father Mario had returned from Italy with a rosary that had been blessed by the pope. He gave this rosary to Father Aloysius to be blessed also by him. Father took the rosary and left the room either to go to his own room or to the chapel. In a few minutes, he returned and without any fore knowledge, told Father Mario the blessings that were already on the rosary.

Chapter Ten

Father Kevin Manion

Certainly a most significant figure in the life of Father Aloysius was Father Kevin Pius Manion who was his secretary for the last eight years of his life. We knew Father Kevin as a special companion and assistant when he was a layman engaged in commercial enterprises. On a Sunday afternoon when Father wished to visit us in Alta Loma, Kevin would be his driver for the ninety mile round trip. It made my wife Mary and me very happy to be able to provide a home meal and a quiet restful environment for Father to enjoy. In fact, at a later date, when any seminarian from Alamos, Mexico where Father's Foundation had its home would come to visit us, we referred to our house as La Casa del Norte (The House of the North).

A visit to our home would be enhanced sometimes by a few piano selections by Kevin who always seemed to enjoy the afternoons as much as Father did.

It was many years later, on April 11, 1997 when Mary and I were in San Antonio, Texas that we were able to interview Father Kevin at Immaculate Heart of Mary Church. How significant a location, since it is the very place that had been Father Aloysius' assignment from 1966 to 1969. Here he had been the Superior and Pastor at the Mother House of the Claretians. For the material transformation that Father Aloysius had made in the parish, the city bestowed on him three awards. The landscaping of the grounds and the remodeling of the Church and rectory were the special achievements which

51

were being acknowledged. Father Aloysius attributed much of his success in this parish to Father Patrick McPolin and Father Marcel Salinas. In fact, it was at the suggestion of Father Aloysius to the Provincial that Father Salinas be brought from Fort Worth for the Cursillo Movement.

Today, Father Kevin is enthusiastically engaged in furthering the knowledge of the life of Father Aloysius. In addition to his duties in his parish assignment in San Marcos, Texas, Father Kevin is conserving no energy in expounding the life and spirituality of his holy mentor. When the day finally arrives when by the will of God, Father Aloysius becomes canonized, it will be to no small part attributable to the efforts of Father Kevin.

At some time before Father Aloysius made his Foundation in Mexico at Alamos, Sonora, the Bishop that he dealt with had a very good friend named Juan Jesus Posadas Ocampo who was the Bishop of Tijuana. Bishop Ocampo was also well know to Father Kevin and later became the Bishop of Cuernavaca. When he was named to be the Archbishop of Guadalajara, he chose Father Kevin to accompany him on his trip to Rome where he was invested as a Cardinal. Most tragically, on May 24, 1993, Cardinal Ocampo was shot to death by fourteen bullets at close range at the airport. A government inquiry stated that the Cardinal was the victim of a shootout as he was caught in the middle of a gunfight between rival cocaine cartels who mistakenly identified him as a drug lord. The Catholic Church lost a Cardinal and Father Kevin lost a close friend.

In his interview, Father Kevin is definitive in the responses which Father Aloysius gave to the questions about certain mystical gifts given to him. Regarding special odors or the ability to bi-locate, while not denying them, Father Aloysius simply was not aware of these occurrences. He stated that it may have been his guardian angel that had appeared for him. Father Kevin explained how anxious people are to proclaim these phenomena that we might even say that they become fanatical. "There was a fringe element of people who were so looking for extraordinary signs that they would see them even though they may not have existed." However it was evident on numerous occasions that Father did possess the ability to read souls.

Father Kevin was emphatic in his description of Father's spirituality. This characteristic was clear and obvious. He saw the Hand of God in every work and he was always aware of the Divine Presence so that he constantly walked with the Lord. Father Kevin's words are: "Father's basic spirituality was such that when he came into a room, we all knew that someone special had come in, just by his presence. It's not that he had a commanding personality. He was so close to God, in communion with God. He actually was another Jesus Christ among us. I think that he fulfilled what the Gospel has asked all of us to follow. Father Aloysius was in a sense on Mount Tabor communicating with Almighty God and in the world being with us." Father Kevin felt that Father Aloysius touched us all in that we were aware of a special connection between him and the transcending God. Father Kevin speaks of Father Aloysius' spirituality as being unique and so special and sometimes so simple and clear.

As Father's driver, Father Kevin noticed the facility with which this task was accomplished: something that others too, like myself have experienced. It was common practice to say three to fifteen Rosaries during a trip. Father Kevin feels that it was the efficacy of the Holy Rosary that brought about such easy trips. The regimen for one funeral was described in this manner: "One time we were driving, (it) may have been way out in West Covina or some other place in downtown Los Angeles, we would say three Rosaries going (there) and coming back; maybe (we would say) one Rosary en route, as we were trying to find the (church) and one Rosary coming back (from the church). And I think there was once when he said fifteen Rosaries. I think part of the secret to Father Aloysius' spirituality was his great dedication to the Rosary and to the Blessed Sacrament."

When I spoke to Fr. Kevin asking if he had heard of any events after Father's death that could relate to his spirituality, he said: You might see some pictures which show that he had what "...looks like the Blessed Sacrament or a glow right in the center of his forehead or some other place."

In this interview we learn that Father came back from his two years in Fatima "as a broken person." How fortunate it is that at this time, in 1973, when he was in such need that Father Kevin was to begin his span of eight years as chauffer and secretary. I remember well this era when I myself saw him and was able to help him at a reception. When he greeted the crowd that awaited him at his first public appearance, he was fully composed and effusive. His graciousness was unbounded and the devotion of the people had not waned. We could never sense what difficulties had beset him during his efforts to launch his new Foundation while in Europe.

One particular event that is most interesting occurred at a benefit dinner which Father Aloysius attended. The story is related by Father Kevin as follows:

"When I was working as Father Aloysius' secretary, this would have been about the year 1975, probably shortly before Father Thomas Matin took the pilgrimage to Europe where he subsequently died, there was a benefit for Father Thomas Matin or the Claretian priests at Baroni's Restaurant on Riverside Drive in Toluca Lake. He had invited about, I think they were supposed to sell tickets for about a hundred or a hundred and twenty. And sure enough Father Thomas Matin ended up telling everybody to come. So there were probably about 170 people there, almost double the amount they were expecting. Now during this particular benefit dinner there were some door prizes that were awarded. And I brought Father Aloysius to Baroni's Restaurant. He was sitting in the back of the restaurant in the banquet room at one of the tables. And at the time of the door prize it was Connie Vrondran, Joe and Connie Vrondran's daughter, I believe it was Terri or it could have been Toni Vrondran who actually picked the numbers out of the hat or whatever it was to award the people the door prizes. She picked the first number out and she read the number. A person received their door prize and then she picked another number out and the person received their door prize. When the Vrondran daughter picked the third number out, she read the number. It was like number one twenty three. And from the back of the room where I was sitting with Father Aloysius, he stood up and he yelled to the front; he said: 'That's a mistake, read the number over again.' And so the little girl looked at the number she had picked out and she read it again. Sure enough, she had made a mistake and she read the correct number, which may have been an inversion of the numbers, one thirty two or whatever it was. And so, Father Aloysius came up to receive his door prize. He said when he got up to the microphone: 'I prayed to St. Michael, the Archangel to let me win this last door prize because he has never let me down and I wanted to share with everyone some of the extraordinary things that St. Michael has done in my life. And so in thanksgiving to St. Michael the Archangel, I am very happy to receive this door prize.'"

Chapter Eleven

Connie Vorndran

Connie Vorndran and her husband Joe were most faithful as staunch supporters of Father Aloysius. I observed them particularly in their participation in the Guilds which Father had established. In fact, Joe was the president of all the Guilds. Joe was a unique figure among scientists of this age. He was so humble and engaging that you could hardly believe that he was a chief scientist with Hughes Aircraft Co. It was a long time before I myself learned this fact.

However, absolutely nothing was more important to Joe and Connie than the ardent practice of their Faith. Their example was a brilliant beacon to all and could not have shined brighter than during their ordeal with their own disabled daughter. As in many cases, it was during this trial that Our Blessed Lord provided assistance through His holy servant Father Aloysius. And it is through Father's participation in the family trial that we learn a profound lesson in compassion. This deep concern which Father exhibited so very many times in his ministering to the sick and needy was absolutely a display of virtue of the highest.

In July of 1957, a little girl was born to Joe and Connie. This, their second child, Maureen Elizabeth unfortunately was born blind. Obviously this was a very upsetting situation which had been caused by the fact that during the first six weeks of Connie's pregnancy, her other daughter had contracted German Measles. And Connie in turn also contracted measles.

Aloysius

One day while Joe and Connie were with Maureen in a religious store in Culver City they met a woman who immediately proclaimed: "What a beautiful baby." When she found out that this beautiful child could not see, she was quick to say that she knew Father Aloysius and that Joe and Connie should go to see him and take their baby to him.

At the first opportunity to attend the Sunday Novena at the Claretian Provincial House, the Vorndrans brought their daughter Maureen to see Father Aloysius. But it was so crowded in the parlor and the adjoining chapel that it was apparently too stuffy for the little baby. So Joe and Connie brought her outside and sat under a tree for fresh air and shade. Not too long after, Father Aloysius himself came out from the small chapel through all of the people who had been in prayer. Father walked over by the tree and addressed them: "Come, I've been waiting for you." Then he took them past the large crowd that had been waiting for his blessing and brought them into the chapel. After he prayed intently for Maureen in a display of great affection and love, Father walked them out to their car. He said that he was going to offer everything for Maureen.

The next day, when Father spoke to Connie, he said: "First of all, I must tell you, your husband has the soul of St. Joseph. I have never known a soul that was more like St. Joseph." Several times a week Maureen was brought to visit with Father during the month of November 1957. Connie relates that during the course of these visits, Father told them that they were predestined souls and that Maureen would be able to see on Christmas day.

Aloysius

As had been foretold, Maureen received her sight on Christmas day. This fact was proven by Maureen smiling and following the motion of a little stuffed animal as it was moved around. Previously, her large beautiful eyes had been open but unable to see. The doctor said that he had never seen such large eyes before.

It wasn't long before Joe and Connie learned that Maureen had a large hole in her heart. Father Aloysius wanted Joe and Connie to take the baby to see a heart specialist because he had been praying so hard for her that he knew her heart had been healed. When they followed Father's advice and saw a heart specialist in Pasadena, he said that this child's heart is perfect.

Some days later, sadness again beset Joe and Connie when they went to see their pediatrician. This doctor announced that the baby's heart was the same as before. And soon it became necessary to hospitalize her when she caught the flu from her older sister Terri. Now it was January and after being admitted to the hospital, the doctor predicted that Maureen would not survive this illness. Joe and Connie spent long hours with Maureen and then phoned Father Aloysius. When he got the news, Father wanted to go to the hospital immediately, so Joe picked him up at the Provincial House. Upon arrival at the Children's Hospital, they were greeted by the doctor who told them: "I'm sorry, your child is gone." At this announcement, Father put his head down and said: "Pray for this one man, he has no faith." This was a very kind Jewish doctor who regretted it whenever he had to give a shot to Maureen. The tears would flow down his cheeks because he didn't want to hurt her.

After Maureen died, Father Aloysius wanted to pray for her to come back to life but he had the strongest temptation not to do so. In death, Maureen's hands were clasped such that Father said she was grasping the merits of eternal salvation. He said: "I could pray for her to come back, but if you could see her glory and her happiness, you wouldn't."

At the Rosary for Maureen, Father stated that every person at that Rosary would have eternal salvation through her. He said that the angels dressed her. Previously, Father had told Joe and Connie that Maureen was not an ordinary soul. She was destined from all eternity to do her work from heaven.

Father used to speak freely about Maureen and then after a while he stopped doing so because he said there was too much jealousy. And Connie remembered one incident when a lady came up to her after a guild meeting and asked if it were true that Father had said Maureen Elizabeth received infinite graces at Baptism: way more than an ordinary child? And Father said: "Yes, I did say that . It is true." He made it loud and clear.

Father told Joe and Connie on more than one occasion that Maureen was his second angel. She never left his side and he gave her many things to do for him. When Father returned home from one of his trips, and was being brought to a welcoming home dinner, though he was suffering from a very, very bad chest cold, he said: "I go nowhere until I have been to see Maureen Elizabeth." When one of the ladies admonished him, he repeated: "I go nowhere until I have been to see

Maureen." The entourage with him then proceeded to the cemetery. As Father lay prostrate on Maureen's grave, he dedicated his ministry back in Los Angeles again to her and asked her to guard and protect him from the devil and to watch over him.

At one time, Father Aloysius visited the Vorndran's home to conduct the Guild Meetings that he led. Father stated that God was in that house and Father blessed it so that it would never be burglarized or intruded. Of course, this gave a great feeling of security to Connie especially on the occasion when one of her neighbors spotted two men coming up to the front door and they immediately left. They proceeded to go next door to burglarize that house.

Connie had a difficult time in pregnancies and summarized after Maureen's death that her difficulties would continue. However, during a visit that Father Aloysius made to their house, Connie told him they were considering adopting a baby. When Father heard this, he replied: "No, you're going to have a baby." And so they did. On January 20, 1960, exactly two years after Maureen's death, the baby arrived. In order to fulfill a promise to name the child after St. Anthony Mary Claret, Joe and Connie named her Antonia. Later, they referred to her as Tony. On the anniversary of Maureen's death, when Tony was a year old, she developed the croup as had been the case with her older sisters. Joe worked with the child, using steam in the shower while Connie called the doctor and Father Aloysius. Because of his experience with prank calls, Father was a bit reluctant to answer the phone at four in the morning. Fortunately, he did answer it and instructed Connie to say the Rosary. Also, she was to bring Joe some holy water and St.

Anthony Mary Claret's relic. While Joe was to put the holy water in Tony's mouth, Father would be saying the Rosary with Connie over the phone. Just as Tony was starting to get better, they got to the fifth mystery and the doorbell rang. Father told Connie to let the doctor in while he continued to pray the mystery. When the doctor saw the baby, he said: "It's a miracle." And so thereafter, whenever Father saw Tony, he called her the "Miracle of the Rosary." On this, Maureen's feast day, Father said he had begged Maureen to spare her sister.

As time passed, Father died and Tony grew older, she had dreams wherein Father instructed her to pray the Rosary because he said: "Remember, you are the 'Miracle of the Rosary.'" I asked Connie to tell me when these dreams had occurred. She said: "Just after he died."

During the time that Joe and Connie were attending the Sunday afternoon novenas at the Claretian Provincial House, there was one particular Sunday when Connie was not able to accompany Joe and their daughter Theresa because she was in great pain. When Father became aware of Connie's absence, he made certain to inquire as to Connie's dilemma. He then instructed Joe to have Connie phone him when he arrived home. The phone call which Connie made proved to be of no avail. This was obvious after Father had repeatedly blessed Connie with no tangible results. However, Connie was able to fall asleep. Soon thereafter, she awakened with a start and sat up to view St. Anthony Mary Claret standing at the foot of the bed. He spoke not a word but only smiled. By the time that Connie had awakened Joe, St. Anthony was no longer there. Connie however, was absolutely convinced of his visit and definitely benefitted by it as she now was completely free of her excruciating pain. She never had a vision before; nor has she had one since. When she related this incident to Father Aloysius, his reaction was to look downward and smile.

Connie stated that Father Aloysius did not have the practice of blessing the public until the day when a young blind boy from the East was visiting and almost immediately recovered his sight when he had been blessed. When Father called the other priests in the house to witness the result of this blessing, it is thought by Connie that he was now allowed to give public blessings.

As is the case with many interviews, extended conversation brings out more recollections such as the time when Father told her that one day we would all be under the banner of St. Anthony Mary Claret in heaven. When I inquired about Father's sanctity, she described his unique ability to speak of Our Lord and the Blessed Mother in such a manner so that the words would stay with you. Whereas, had these same words been spoken by someone else, even another priest, you could forget them the next day. He made our faith come alive. He made sacrifices as was the incident one night at Connie's Guild meeting when Father said the Rosary while kneeling on the grill of the floor furnace, a spot that was available in the crowded room. And his sacrifice for others was exhibited once when he blessed Maureen and said: "You could go home in peace; this child will not suffer another pain." Connie knew then that Father had taken on her suffering himself. And that's what he did for many others. Another example cited by Connie was the time at a Guild meeting when Father appeared exhausted;

he looked terrible. It was then that he had brought back a "big fish"----a big sinner.

Connie's father apparently had a relationship with Father Aloysius. He died just two hours after Father's death. Previously, Father had told Connie her father would not die until the time that he would go straight to heaven. Thus, Connie believes that Father carried him there on his coattails.

Father Aloysius had also told Joe and Connie about his gift of retention of the Sacred Species wherein he constantly had the Holy Eucharist within himself. And he expanded this information by saying that he had also been given "all the gifts." Having been given this information and also through her own experience during Father's visits, she believed that he could read souls. Her evidence was his demeanor and conversation with her and Joe. Particularly was she impressed when she cited this incident: One day, Father Aloysius had to hear confessions in a nearby parish and he requested that Joe drive him there. Gladly, Joe complied and then later brought Father back to their house. On this occasion, Joe said: "Father, because we're trying to sanctify our lives and do better----you never said you could see our souls----could you just tell us what in our lives is displeasing to God?" And it was obvious that Father did not want to tell them. But finally he conceded, after Connie had begged him. Father's reply was: "Your lack of gratitude." They both realized then that we take a lot of graces and gifts for granted and we don't appreciate them.

Connie who had two brothers and two sisters was very close to her sister Mary from the time of their childhood.

Mary died in 1991 after very painful cancer and its related surgeries, Mary's life was an excellent example of devotion to Our Lady and the subsequent blessings. After the initial spinal surgery and shortly before the final and radical surgery, Our Blessed Mother appeared to her and filled her with peace and joy. She was radiant and happy.

Joe Vorndran was a man of great discipline and fortitude. His father died when he was twelve and his mother was left with five children. The youngest was four, then they were six, eight, twelve and fourteen. He was the second oldest and was the only boy. The family lived in a lovely house that the father, a stone mason, had built. But they were very poor. When the father died, the mother had to go to work. And Joe at his young age, and on his own, took responsibility and went to work also. He did hard physical work on a farm and later worked in a coffee shop every night until midnight. He was a most thoughtful brother in that he used his earnings from farm work to provide things for his sisters. His earnings at the coffee shop were saved for his college education. He was able to get through the lower grades through a scholarship which he was given to the Aquinas Institute. When Joe was working in the coffee shop till midnight, he rode his bicycle all the way to the suburbs where he lived, about seven miles. When he got home at night, he did his homework and maintained a straight A average for four years and never was tardy or absent. This is most remarkable when you consider that his transportation was a bicycle and the area that he lived in was Rochester with its cold climate. He was given awards for being the outstanding scholar in German and Latin.

The unique qualities which Joe possessed tended to serve him and others very well indeed. When Father led a tour to various shrines in Europe in 1968, Joe Vorndran was the one who organized the events. This was a very difficult task to accomplish because Father was so intent on visiting numerous sites and to accommodate Father's frequent change in plans, Joe had to redo his itinerary. Obviously, Joe was just the right man for this task. He was an engineering graduate of the Massachusetts Institute of Technology and Chief Scientist for Hughes Aircraft where he had been for thirty years. He proved to be a great organizer.

Not long after the pilgrimage, during a routine physical examination, Joe learned that he had a liver problem. At the time of discovery it was not serious but as time progressed so did the ailment which was termed chronic hepatitis. He was resigned to his illness and willingly accepted it.

Joe helped Fr. Aloysius in every way possible and when Father did not require the same degree of assistance, Joe turned his efforts toward aiding Fr. Thomas Matin. This priest was a hard working provider for those who were unable to afford seminary training. He built San Conrado Mission in Los Angeles in 1966 and was known as the Saint of Bouett St. Among his parishioners he had built a reputation as a holy man. As he was leading a pilgrimage to Europe in 1975, Fr. Matin died while on his visit to Lourdes.

Joe Vorndran fought his illness for five years but it proved to be a losing battle. On the night of October 24, 1983, a priest came to visit him. Connie did not know this priest for she had never met him. When he entered the sick room at eleven o'clock at night, he said: "I come in the name of Father Thomas Matin. Soon Joseph you are going to be seeing Our Blessed Mother, aren't you happy?" Joe looked up at the priest with a smile and said: "Oh, yeah." Then, the priest continued: "Will you remember this poor priest when you are in heaven?" Although very weak, but fully conscious, Joe replied: "Oh, yes, I will." During that night, he went into a coma. In the morning, and for the rest of the day, the family gathered around him praying the Rosary. Obviously, Joe was unable to respond until suddenly he said "Holy Mary, Mother of God, pray for us sinners now and at the hour of our death." Right beside the bed, Terri, the oldest daughter, while holding Joe's hand, prayed to Maureen, her little sister in heaven: "Please give Mommy a sign. Let Mama have a sign that's going to be a consolation." Connie stood with her eyes closed as Terri said: "Mom, look at Daddy smile." As the corners of Joe's lips moved up and his eyes opened, Joe smiled. Connie stated that his whole face was radiant as though he were a youth of twenty years. It was as though he were viewing a whole panorama, like he was in ecstasy. The nurse and a visiting priest witnessed this event along with the family. He finally succumbed on October 25, 1983 which was two years after the death of Father Aloysius. Shortly after he died, there was a friend who with a bishop had raced to the house to see Joe but they arrived too late, Joe had just died. She and the bishop went into the room. As he came out, the bishop said: "He's not dead, he's alive. He is bathed in light."

Chapter Twelve

Father Frank Ambrosi, C.M.F.

Father Frank Ambrosi was one of the Claretian priests who resided at the Provincial House in Los Angeles in the early sixties. He was a very practical, energetic and holy man, tireless in his efforts to aid anyone in need. He came to the Seminary after a tour of duty in the Army and had numerous doubts about his true vocation. At first, finding himself in a diocesan seminary environment, he happily shifted to the Claretians when he heard that they were all about serving in the foreign missions and most importantly that the Claretians had been given a promise from heaven of eternal salvation through their founder, St. Anthony Mary Claret.

During Father Ambrosi's time in the Seminary, Father Aloysius was a constant source of encouragement with such phrases as: "Oh my boy, you're doing so good. Keep up your good prayers." Such friendly and informal conversations assured him of the possibility of fulfilling his dream of becoming a Missionary. "Yes, my dear boy, you could be a good Missionary in our order." And even in Fr. Ambrosi's desire to do gardening, he was encouraged to continue this hobby. At one time, Fr. Ambrosi became a bit disconsolate as he was reading the lives of the saints. He related his concern by saying: "Father, this is too much---all these virtues you're supposed to have---I don't find one of them in my life." But a few simple very compassionate words put him back at ease. This utmost compassion of Father Aloysius was exhibited over and over again such as the time that one of the older priests was experiencing obvious distress from extreme loneliness. His painful and tearful wails could be heard as he paced the floor. How wonderful it was that Father Aloysius was close at hand to render assistance and restore peace to this poor suffering priest.

Father Aloysius was great at saving vocations both before and after ordination. During this era of church history, there was a rather strong demand for adherence to a more rigid discipline. When confronting such a requirement in the Seminary after having previously been in a more carefree environment, it sometime proved to be a daunting task for the young seminarians. If you couldn't adjust to the standards, you'd be out. What a life saver Father Aloysius proved to be when his compassionate words were just the right elixir for continuation with your God given calling to the priesthood. Even in the simpler cases, the loving and forgiving nature of Father Aloysius was put into practice when minor disciplinary rules were broken such as eating "goodies" after hours or failing to turn off the lights on time. To describe Father Aloysius' attitude, Father Ambrosi put it simply when he said the Novices were not expected to be confirmed priests or Missionaries. Father Aloysius saw to it that proper recreation was provided and even during these times, he himself when approached by a seminarian was always available for mini conferences on the playing field. He could create an eventful trip when there was none scheduled just like the time that he staged a tree trimming for the boys so that they could take a trip in a borrowed truck to Gardena to dump the trimmings. They would even have a little picnic treat along the way. Father Ambrosi remembered the picnics that were provided by and accompanied by Father Aloysius as he strode along the field saying his Divine Office.

At about eight o'clock at night it became time for Father Aloysius to become the Spiritual Director for the young trainees. After a very busy day he would give his well prepared talks. This was a critical time in their life and he was certainly up to the task of giving the needed direction. Even when not directly instructing, his actions preached a resounding example. He was a very self sacrificing man as was evidenced by the ongoing interruptions which he experienced when called to console visitors or when there was need to pray with the sick and dying on the unending telephone calls which he received. Yet, no matter what the hour, if the day had slipped by without the opportunity to say the Divine Office, Father would reach into the night hours to fulfill this obligation.

All of the attributes which Father Ambrosi witnessed in Father Aloysius had a profound effect on him. One of these qualities, Father Ambrosi was emphatic to admit: the Divine Office was not to be omitted unless the underlying circumstances were absolutely impossible.

During his Seminary life, Father Ambrosi was present to see the compassion and love for the masses of people who came to him for whatever need there was. His words would be: "We must ask God with faith." And he would also say: "We are not worthy of miracles." He helped a countless number of families to be reconciled with God. His love even extended out to the religious articles which they brought to him to be blessed. This was far from a cursory procedure and always accompanied with holy water as many others will concede.

How very well Father Ambrosi remembered all of the incidences of priestly devotion that were set by his mentor. Great attention was always given to prayer at all times of the day. To illustrate a single example, whenever the circumstances caused the noon prayers to be missed, you could be sure that Father Aloysius could be seen later in the day catching up on the omission. The Holy Rosary, Benediction of the Blessed Sacrament and Holy Hour were absolutely essential practices. Of course, everyone knew that for Father Aloysius, the Holy Sacrifice of the Mass was the crowning achievement of the day.

Like a great coach in some sports endeavor, Father Aloysius stressed the fundamentals of the religious life such as chastity, poverty and obedience. In his instructions, the practical nature of the subject matter and richness of the quotations within left quite an impression. Father Ambrosi was also well aware of the knowledge that Father Aloysius possessed in Latin, Greek and English as he exhibited these qualities in his writing. He was a "pious, intelligent man with a rich source of doctrine." Another attribute was his clerical attire which would attest to his diligence in performance of his duties. His demeanor was self effacing in his word and in his actions. Almighty God was the one and only cause of all gifts. Father Ambrosi described Father Aloysius in a manner that many will remember: "When he would talk, he would always look at you, but he would have his eyes cast down. His conferences were wonderful and well prepared." The virtues of the Blessed Mother and reliance on her Immaculate Heart were stressed. As given to Father Ambrosi, the conferences for the whole month of October were dedicated to the Holy Rosary. "And really it was a treasure." Father Ambrosi was so impressed by all of the conferences that he kept notes of every one. Unfortunately he was not able to retain them as they were borrowed never to be returned.

If there were two saints to be singled out among the very many upon which Father Aloysius modeled his life, they were The Blessed Mother and St. Anthony Mary Claret, the Founder of the Claretians. These were the invocations which were heard from him over and over again in every circumstance of prayer and instruction. The Immaculate Hearts of Jesus and Mary were so prominently displayed in his surroundings.

Many years later, in 1981, Father Frank Ambrosi celebrated the twenty-fifth anniversary of his ordination to the priesthood. During this same year, his mentor, Father Aloysius Ellacuria was called to his eternal reward.

Fr. Aloysius and His brother, Fr. Jose Maria, with their sister, Poli, and her husband and children

Chapter Thirteen

Dorothy Hulen

Some of our interviews were particularly enjoyable because of the closeness to Father Aloysius which they engendered. It wasn't always a story of miraculous events that were related to us; sometimes it was a special relationship that one had with Father. These friendships which we discovered, further illustrated the personal warmth that emanated from this holy priest. Such was the nature of our talk with Dorothy Hulen on January 26, 1991 in Phoenix, Arizona.

Dorothy was a gentle lady of middle age who found herself one day in a totally new environment. She was a long practicing Methodist who was ready to hear the call to conversion when Our Lord provided the scenario.

Dorothy's sister invited her one Sunday to come with their brother Kenneth to pay a visit to Father Aloysius and receive his blessing. In rather routine fashion, Father proceeded with his blessing of the congregation, but when he came to Kenneth, he stopped and said: "You have asthma very bad. Will you please come to my office tomorrow morning at ten o'clock." Thus a relationship with the family was begun.

Father Aloysius was stationed at Immaculate Heart of Mary Church and he had a particularly difficult task on his hands at the time. The church had recently experienced a destructive fire and now was in need of repairs. This task fell into the hands of Father Aloysius the new pastor, and Dorothy was happy to do what she could to help.

At some earlier date, Kenneth had been baptized in Los Angeles, but not so with Dorothy. In an early conversation with Father Aloysius, he said to her: "It won't be long before I will be baptizing you too." Soon thereafter, she began taking instruction at St. Vincent de Paul. She continued her relationship with the Claretians at Immaculate Heart, including Father Ambrosi and Father Salinas who was the assistant pastor.

A schedule had been set up for Dorothy to be baptized on her birthday, December 7, 1963. However, there was a Cursillo for women on that date and Father Aloysius was very busy. Additionally, because of his responsibility to hear confessions, he became unavailable to baptize Dorothy. After waiting for a couple of hours for Father Aloysius, Father Salinas decided to proceed with the baptism. Then on Sunday December 8, 1963, the Feast of the Immaculate Conception, Dorothy Hulen received her First Holy Communion. From then on, a closer relationship developed between Dorothy and Father Aloysius and Kenneth developed a particular friendship.

The influence of Father reached out even further: Dorothy's mother had not been baptized, so by Father Salinas driving, Father Aloysius was able to visit her a lot. And he saw to it that a lay person would give her instruction into the Catholic Faith. At the age of 75, Father Aloysius baptized Dorothy's mother at Immaculate Heart of Mary Church in Phoenix.

For over a year, Dorothy did house cleaning and worked in the kitchen and then started assisting by helping with the donations that came in and writing notes for Father. The next assignment then for Father was to the very old Immaculate Heart of Mary Church in San Antonio. Kenneth accompanied Father on this transfer. Dorothy was able to continue providing secretarial help to Father while she was still in Phoenix and he was in San Antonio. She would write letters for him and send them to Father for signature. Then Father would mail them from San Antonio. Dorothy couldn't help but notice how many cases of miracles and wonderful events were recounted to Father in the correspondence which she handled. Many people were obviously impressed through their association with Father and from the prayers and blessings which he offered. To Dorothy, he was a living saint.

Before we began this interview, Dorothy asked that I go to her garage and help retrieve a box. This box was labeled: "Father Aloysius Pictures." In my mind, I expected to find a few ordinary snapshots. Oh no, that was not the case. Here was a box that was an absolute treasure. Dorothy had amassed a countless array of historical photos of Father: pictures of himself, pictures of his seminarians, pictures of his fellow priests and even some wonderful pictures of his family. Dorothy satisfied my curiosity about this valuable trove when I asked how she had gotten them.

As Father's valued assistant, Dorothy was asked to help when he was transferred from Phoenix to San Antonio. There were many religious paintings, statues and other items to be considered. So, Dorothy contacted a moving company to have these items packed and shipped to San Antonio. At that time, Father gave instructions for her to keep the letters and pictures so that he could get them later. However, as time went on, Father moved from place to place and Dorothy still had the boxes. Then, some time after Father's death, she sent at least two boxes of letters to the Claretian Provincial House in Los Angeles, probably to Father John Martens. Since they only wanted the letters sent to them, Dorothy retained the box of pictures. She knew that someday, someone would come forward and like to have them.

In my effort to learn everything possible about Father Aloysius from Dorothy, I asked: "When you were associated with Father, did you notice any special characteristics about him that made him different from other people. Did he seem different to you from other people?" She was immediate with her reply: "Very much so! He had such an insight into everything and everyone around him, and it seemed almost like he could look right into your mind --- and just like when he said to me the first time he ever met me: 'I will baptize you before this year is over.'" Dorothy provided the final emphasis to her conviction when she stated further: "I hadn't given a thought to being a Catholic." And she continued to relate her impressions when she said: "When you were in his presence, you were in the presence of a very, very holy man. And you could see that when he was at his desk, sitting there, he would close his eyes---you knew he was in deep concentration." Then when Father was ready to deal with the matters at hand, he would come right out of his concentration and state where he was going to go. He was always ready to go to the Cursillos or any other duty that called and: "If required, two hours or twenty hours in the confessional, Father Aloysius was there."

As for Father's individual blessings, Dorothy felt just as so many others did. When he placed his hands on her head, she had a feeling "of full serenity; you felt like every bit of tension was drained right from you."

Besides knowing Father Aloysius so well, Dorothy also had the privilege of a warm association with his brother, Father José, who remained in Phoenix after Father Aloysius had gone to San Antonio and Father José was a frequent visitor to Dorothy's mother. Father José was able to drive and he moved at a rapid pace.

When Father Aloysius moved from San Antonio to Fatima, he was far from his friends in Phoenix and thus Dorothy lost her chance to visit him or have him come to her house as he had done so often in the past. But then when he returned to Los Angeles, and Dorothy's mother died, she was able to speak to him again and at a later date was able to travel to Los Angeles and visit for almost two hours with him.

Dorothy Hulen's acquaintance with Father Aloysius was memorable and continued to be felt after his death, as she stated: "I just feel like he's around. What would he tell me ---how would he tell me to handle this situation? You just really feel it."

Chapter Fourteen

Father Tom Warren

From Sacred Heart Church in Parker, Arizona, Father Tom Warren came to my house for an interview on January 8, 1991. Although still attached to the archdiocese of Los Angeles, he works outside of Los Angeles in the diocese of Tucson. While still in high school Seminary in the Fall of 1953, he first heard of Father Aloysius, this wonderful priest who had many gifts of healing and spiritual direction. After only one semester, Father Warren returned to Santa Maria for Junior College. Toward the end of 1961 he entered the diocesan Seminary in Camarillo, California. But because of this late entry, he had to go to summer school to take some other courses at the University of San Francisco. This long road to the priesthood brought about a great depression in young TomWarren. As he was standing in the foyer of the dormitory, he noticed a rolly-polly priest of about fifty clad in black pants and white shirt who was very, very full of life as he walked along with an accompanying Claretian Brother. Tom asked: "Are you a priest?" He said: "Yes I am; my name is Father Aloysius." "You're Father Aloysius; I've heard about you years ago." Tom replied. And said that after a very pleasant discussion, "Father Aloysius read my mind because I had never seen him before. And Father Aloysius continued by saying: "Do not worry young man, some day you will be a priest and you will do many good things for God and I shall pray for you every day."

After he had been ordained about two years and was sent to a parish, he again saw Fr. Aloysius on an occasion that was very comforting to a family who had lost a little boy of eight to cancer. He was a very holy little boy called Andy Shimmer. At this time, there began extremely meritorious weekly visits by Fr. Warren as he drove a forty-two year old doctor with cancer to see Fr. Aloysius at Westchester Place. This was a great source of comfort to the doctor in his dying days. Another case involved a Deacon friend, Bill Delmonico, who had a daughter of about nine named Annie who was in need of eye surgery. Without telling Father Aloysius about the problem, they went to one of the Guild meetings. As they knelt for the Blessing, Father placed his thumbs on the girl's eyes and said nothing. The next day, when Annie was taken to the hospital they were told that there had been some mistake because "This little girl does not need eye surgery." At this time, Annie resided in Thousand Oaks, California.

Another important characteristic that Father Warren interjected emphatically was the fact that "Father Aloysius was extremely devoted to The Immaculate Heart of Mary." She permeated his life. "Who was more a Missionary Son of the Immaculate Heart of Mary than Father Aloysius?" Asked Father Warren.

Father Warren's mother, Mabel, was also able to accompany him to the Claretian Provincial House in Los Angeles to receive a Blessing. In fact, on one occasion, their experience was so overwhelming that they were fearful of driving home on the freeway because they were both so relaxed.

During the turmoil of the post-council era, Father Aloysius said: "Father Warren, you must be very conservative." To this, Father Warren replied: "Like these arch conservatives?" "No, no." Father responded. "I don't mean conservative in that way. I mean in loyalty to the Holy Father and to the Church." And after he himself has spent twenty-five years in the priesthood, Father Warren says that this advice to remain loyal to the Magisterium of the Church has been a very sustaining factor in his own spiritual life. Again here, he stresses that the devotion to the Immaculate Heart of Mary that was exhibited by Father Aloysius has imbued within himself a very powerful devotion to Our Lady.

Father Aloysius was a great confessor and when we spoke of confession, Father Warren described him as having "A great sense of the mercy of God. It was overflowing generously when he would confess people."

Father Aloysius was an animated man of Basque temperament with great love and sincerity and full of compassion and mercy. This quality was obvious when he ministered to those of great wealth such as Conrad Hilton and those of power, color and creed as well as the "local winos." He remained human even when he was the instrument of miraculous cures. He never tired in his efforts to reach those in need. When he was in extremely bad health, he was still open to everybody. When Father Warren told Father Aloysius: "You work day and night." The response was: "My work is my pleasure." The effectiveness of this great compassion and love for the sick was underscored when Father Wallace said: "I know many young people on dope, dope addicts who are now straight---middle aged people with families and children that were converted back to a good wholesome life by Father's work. Many alcoholics and addicted people are now daily communicants. There are many souls who are still very much alive. Today they are Catholic and very wholesome in the presence of God because of his work." And in regard to his own life, Father Warren states: "I've always very much felt that at a time of great turmoil in my personal life, he was a catalyst to help me to finally persevere and become a priest. So for that I'm grateful."

Both priests and lay people spoke to Fr. Warren about the special gift that Father Aloysius had of Retention of the Sacred Species. Two of the priests that were specifically mentioned in this regard were Father Frank Ambrosi and Father Tim Anderson.

Father Aloysius was loyal to his Claretian Order and obedient to his superiors, giving a beautiful example in this regard when he was ordered to leave the diocese. He was admirable in his adherence to the Holy See, to the Pope and to his Ordinary.

In his final remembrances of Father Aloysius, Father Warren said: "Father told me as a young priest, 'Always Bless people. If you can, always be seen going to confession. It's good for the lay people to see a priest confessing his sins in public.' "

Father Aloysius with his Mother and
his brother, Father Jose

Chapter Fifteen

<u>Mother Marguerite Carter</u>

Interviews were continued on May 1, 1996 in Fallbrook, California at the St. Joseph Carmelite Convent where Mother Marguerite Carter recalled her memories of Father Aloysius many years earlier. We spoke of a period of recuperation for Father in the nineteen sixties when the "out of the way" location of this convent was the ideal setting for recovery and peaceful isolation. At that time, the actual place for Father was not here at St. Joseph's but rather at a nearby facility with more suitable accommodations. I was most fortunate at that time to be allowed to visit Father at that site. Not long thereafter, as a result of the healing therapy, he was back at his priestly work in the Provincial House in Los Angeles.

Today however, we turn the clock back to an earlier era in the life of the Carmelites. When about twenty years of age, Mother Marguerite while still kneeling after Benediction of the Blessed Sacrament, heard a little voice which said: "I want you for my Religious and your reward will be in eternity." Her response to this internal voice was to join the Carmelites and begin her life's work. While stationed in Oklahoma, she heard about Father Aloysius and his power to heal. Even though the exact year of this occurrence had faded from her memory, she spoke of the events of the day with clarity and assurance.

Sister Hildergarde was in the hospital in Oklahoma City with a prognosis of approximately three weeks maximum to live. Even though her doctor had denied permission for her to travel to Los Angeles, Mother Marguerite thought differently concerning the long journey since there was already the expectation of an early death. After the doctor had left the room, she said: "What's the difference, you're going to die anyway. You might as well die in the presence of this holy man." It didn't take Sister Hildergarde long to agree with this plan, so Mother Marguerite proceeded to buy the plane ticket. For a portion of the trip that was by car, there was an additional episode when they met Sister Beatrice, a Franciscan who was dying of cancer of the breast. She too was anxious to see Father Aloysius but knew her chances to be slim since her Reverend Mother didn't like this sort of "healing thing." Mother Marguerite was more than willing to take on another passenger but first she had to put in a call to the Reverend Mother, her friend from school days and make a sales pitch. After a brief conversation, the Reverend Mother gave a conditional approval. "Sister Beatrice can go if you'll also take one other Sister who is ill." Mother Marguerite agreed with this stipulation, added another passenger to the station wagon and proceeded onward.

At the Provincial House, the entourage attended the morning Mass which Father Aloysius said. After Mass, Father directed the Sisters to come up to the front row. First, he blessed Sister Kathleen, the driver, then Mother Marguerite and then he came to Sister Hildergarde who was dying and hadn't eaten for a week. So, he blessed her and then moved on to one of the Franciscan Sisters and blessed her. Then, recalls Mother Marguerite, he said something to the effect that "You are not to be healed for your own welfare." Next, was the second Franciscan

Sister whom he blessed and then told the group to "Come tomorrow morning." And that they did. Now, Sister Hildergarde had shown a bit of improvement. Then, the next morning after Mass while they were walking up to the main building from the Chapel, Father said to Mother Marguerite: "She is full of God's love and simplicity." As he referred to Sister Beatrice. This must have been pleasing to her ears since she had not asked for much during her journey. Mother Marguerite remembers the only words Sister had spoken during the trip: "I don't want to be cured, but if it is the Lord's Will, fine. All I want to hear is that I am holy and pleasing in the sight of God." But, Father's consoling statement to Sister Beatrice about being full of God's love and simplicity didn't end there because as he continued talking, he said: "And oh, how holy and pleasing she is in the sight of God." These exact words immediately jogged Mother Marguerite's memory as she recalled the only words Sister Beatrice had spoken on the journey. Now, she was hearing these same words again but this time they were being spoken by Father Aloysius.

Continuing with Sister Hildergarde, Father said: "Go ahead and begin eating." Surely, this seemed necessary since she hadn't eaten for many days. With that advice, the Sisters went down on the seacoast some place and told Sister: "Get what you'd like; he said you can eat." And that she did. She ordered a seafood platter! And she ate every bit of it! When I asked Mother Marguerite if Sister had shared anything, I was told that she was too hungry to share her meal. Somewhat alarmed, Mother Marguerite proclaimed: "Oh, I'm going to be up all night with her. God forgive me."

On the next day, they went back to Father's Mass and after he blessed her he said: "Now, how do you feel?" She replied: "I feel fine." She had been cured! This fact was later proven by hospital x-rays back home in Oklahoma.

The second Franciscan, whom the Reverend Mother had stipulated be a member of the trip, was a person who had difficulty getting along with people. When Father blessed her, he told her that she would be better but she would not be cured. When she went home, she became a different person entirely. People could live with her; they could put up with her. So, she went back to the hospital where she was the head of some department.

When Sister Beatrice returned to Oklahoma City, "She went to the x-ray department, it happened that she was the head of the x-ray department, and she had her picture taken. There was no cancer. None! So, when her doctor came in later on, she said: 'Would you like to take a picture of me?' 'Yes, he said.' 'Where's your cancer? There's no cancer now.' She had been cured."

Succinctly, Mother Marguerite sums up the episode with:"Those who were to be cured were to be cured."

To me, this entire situation was most interesting because I recall having had a conversation with Father Aloysius wherein he spoke of Nuns from Oklahoma coming out to California to see him. Now, at last I learned of the happy details of that trip.

There were surely several other interesting events that were related by Mother Marguerite. All of the details were not available but the essentials were certainly now to be relived. Mother did not recall any special aroma that may have been experienced when in Father's presence but she was quick to tell of his levitation as she stated: "I saw him levitate; we were on a tour of Europe...and we had come to the Sisters of Charity. Father was going to say Mass there." This location about which she spoke is well known. It is the beautiful Chapel on Rue de Bac in Paris where the Daughters of Charity of St. Vincent de Paul are stationed. In this sanctuary in 1830, Our Blessed Mother appeared to Sister Catherine Labouré with the design for her famous Miraculous Medal. When my wife, Mary and I visited this area in 1979 we were unable to enter because of extensive repairs that were underway. Even the chair upon which Our Blessed Lady sat is still preserved and was seen there by Mother Marguerite.

On the day that Father Aloysius was to say Mass, he had to move to an adjacent altar because of scheduling difficulties. Mother Marguerite describes the event as: "We went up there, and as he was saying Mass, when he came to the Consecration, he put out his arms and he began to levitate. I'd say he levitated about six inches at least. And he said, as he levitated: 'My God, keep thy arms up; don't let them fall.' Then he went back."

At least one other woman witnessed this episode; she was doctor Jean O'Donnell who was part of the contingent on this European tour. A Spanish nun, Mother Esperanza, who was a friend of Father, met doctor O'Donnell at this time and told her: "You are going to be a Sister." This prophesy came to fulfillment some time later when Jean O'Donnell became a Trappist Nun.

I asked Mother Marguerite to speak of Father's blessings as she had known them. She said: "He blessed me with a monstrance one day and he thought he would cure me, but I wasn't cured. So he came back to me and said: 'You are not to be cured. You are to live for the salvation of souls.'"

Does Mother Marguerite pray to Father? "Yes," She says. "I pray to him; I have prayed to him; I pray to him every day. His picture is outside my door and then the picture that hung over his bed is on the side of my wall. So, I talk to him very often."

Some years after Father had died, there was another tour taken by Mother Marguerite to a town in Mexico as she was a guest of Rita Murphy who was another very good friend of Father Aloysius. "I was the last one to come out of the Church there. A lady who had since passed away had given Mother Marguerite forty dollars to be given to the poor. The opportunity to perform this act of charity presented itself when Mother became the last person to leave the Chapel. She says: "I was tickled to death; now, I could stay after the others were gone and give the money out to these little old mothers that were there with all these children." When her mission had been completed, she went to return to the bus. "And as I did," she continued, "I saw that the bus was located at the top of a hill; and coming down the hill, in the street, was water; just gushing. So, I said I'll never be able to go up there. And then I looked at the sidewalk......the only place I could get to it was about three feet tall; and I said I don't know how I'll ever get that either. So, I said, I've got to try. I kept going and I thought, I could get on my stomach....throw myself on my stomach and turn around and get up....the only way I could think." However she managed to proceed on her own, was of little consequence because she continued: "Someone took me by the arm and then with that, I turned around and saw this man because his face was even with mine. And then, he went on. The next thing I knew, I was up on the sidewalk. I went to turn around to thank him and there was no one there. That was Father Aloysius." "You're sure it was he?" I asked. "Positive." She replied. I asked further: "This is after he died?" "Oh, yes." She assured me. She didn't know the exact date, but once again she assured me that she was positive the event occurred after Father's death.

Very often during the course of an interview, the conversation will vacillate between different eras of time. Because of the emphasis that is intended in that interview it is sometimes effective to relate the episodes as they are presented during the conversation even though they are not chronologically in sequence. Such is the case when talking to Mother Marguerite. At the time the Carmelite Sisters were caring for Father Aloysius as he was recovering from hip surgery, Mother Marguerite speaks as follows: "He was in bed and he wanted to be raised up, so he asked me to raise his head. I thought to myself, how in the world will I raise his head. He's such a big man; I don't know how I can do that. But again, I'll have to try. So, I put my hand out and before I could get it under the pillow, he had been taken by the Angels and sat up straight."

Animals also were the recipients of Father's blessings as Mother Marguerite re-tells the story she witnessed. At an orphanage in Mexico, near the border, a Passionist Priest was working. One day when he was not at home, there was a hippie, replete with braids tied back. Father Aloysius said to the hippie: "Come over here; you don't believe in God but I'll show you there is a God. Bring that dog over here." It happened, that this dog had three good legs and one that couldn't be put on the ground. The leg was crooked and showed no life. The hippie brought the dog over and Father prayed over the leg as he rubbed it. When he placed the dog back on the ground again, he had four good legs! This prompted Mother Marguerite to exclaim: "I don't know whether the hippie ever believed in God but he should have."

During one of the visits which Mother Marguerite had with Father, he told her of the awesome privilege given to him whereby he had the Holy Eucharist present within him continually.This miracle had also been told to others. Emphatically, I avow to this revelation myself because it was told to me personally by Father in 1961. As our Faith teaches us, we are in a constant battle with the forces of evil. One person whom we should expect to be targeted for harassment by the devil would be Father Aloysius. Mother Marguerite verifies this as follows: "He would come to our house in San Diego on Saturday and stay overnight since he was caring for one of his Guilds in that area. His routine on Sunday was to say Mass then have breakfast and lunch and depart in the afternoon. On one of these visits, he had asked the Sisters to pray that he might bring a seventy year old man back to the Faith. The prayer was answered as it had been requested and that same night, Sister Frances who slept in the room above Father heard "fighting, talking and smashing at things." She became so frightened that she left her room and went down to the Chapel where she slept for the night. That next morning, Father came to his door and said that it was impossible for him to say Mass at the scheduled time; instead he would say it maybe at eleven; which he did. Later on, when the Sisters went to tidy up his room, they found that the glass that was on the pictures in the room had been broken and the sheets and pajamas were both wringing wet. Sister Frances concluded that the noises she heard were made by the devil trying to strangle Father and then Father talking back to him. It was not possible now for us to speak with Sister Frances since she died in April 1996.

Mother Marguerite says that Father Aloysius suggested we should start a Community here in California. Thus, because of this invitation by Father Aloysius, Mother Marguerite considers him to be the Founder of this Community. And during its early days, she felt that the force of the devil was evident on the occasion that the Bishop came to give the first Habit to the Sisters. On that day, a bust of Junipero Serra exhibited great heat and disfigurement when this bust was taken over by the devil and displayed bloodshot eyes and a mouth with a horrible leer. This was experienced by Mother Marguerite and Sister Dorothy.

When questioned about Father Aloysius bi-locating, Mother Marguerite recalled an occasion when Sister Mary had leukemia at Baptist Hospital in Boston and was thought to be just hours away from death. Mother Marguerite was requested to come. Yes, she would do so, but first she would call Father Aloysius who was in Los Angeles and ask for prayers. Assuredly, Father responded: "She will be all right." Then Mother proceeded to

Boston to find Sister Mary looking terrible. "Her face was just like a corpse," said Mother. That night, while she was lying in bed, Father Aloysius appeared to Sister Mary from outside on a piazza. He bowed to her and smiled. Up until this time she hadn't been able to sleep or take medicine. However, the next morning, she was able to take a little bit of food. On the following night, Father returned and did the same thing as before. Bowing and smiling. The next morning, Sister Mary was able to take her medicine. On the third morning, she went home and lived for fifteen more years. Not only did Sister Mary see Father Aloysius, but several cousins of Mother Marguerite saw him as well.

When we spoke to Sister Mary Michael along with Mother Marguerite, Sister Mary Michael told of seeing a broken salt shaker, as though cut in half. This being the result of an exploding salt shaker that seemed to sense the presence of Father Aloysius who made use of salt when he blessed holy water.

Mother Marguerite Carter, after spending many years as a Superior in her Carmelite Community, was moved in later years to Santa Teresita Hospital in Duarte, California where she died.

Father Aloysius Ellacuria, C.M.F

Chapter Sixteen

Father Alberto Ruiz, C.M.F.

In the same setting as the interview with Father Frank Ambrosi, on January 25, 1991, it was a pleasure to talk with Father Alberto Ruiz who just seven weeks earlier had celebrated his sixth anniversary as a Claretian Missionary. Being a delayed vocation, he had been ordained at the age of thirty-nine. When he had received his calling to the priesthood through the Cursillo Movement but yet had to make a decision between entering a diocesan or a Religious Seminary, Father Ambrosi came to his aid. At this time, while he was a Novice in the Seminary, Alberto heard Father Ambrosi speak of Father Aloysius as being a very holy priest and Father Ambrosi sought to provide an introduction to him. Doubtful as to what he should expect from such a meeting, Alberto was hesitant. But, through Father Ambrosi, this meeting did take place. However it was very unsettling to Alberto because his opinion of holiness didn't seem to be exemplified in the comment which Father Aloysius made at a breakfast one morning in the presence of the provincial, other priests and Alberto's parents. Alberto was taken aback when Father Aloysius queried him somewhat as follows: "Why do all you Mexicans wear mustaches?" He was crushed as he thought: "Why could someone who was holy say those things?" Feeling quite sassy, his response to Father Aloysius was: "Jesus had a mustache and long hair." Then, as time moved on and the same group sat down for lunch, Father Aloysius said something to the effect that: "Oh, you don't look so bad; that doesn't look so bad on you." This statement brought about a completely different feeling within Alberto because he now began to feel the humanness of that saintly person. He described this new feeling by saying: "As holy as one might become on earth, the humanness never leaves you. In fact you don't become a saint without your humanness." At this time, Alberto didn't think he would see Father Aloysius again and he also didn't think he would become a Claretian. Yet, his whole idea of a priestly vocation was to be brought about through the Claretians. One morning in 1979, when he had gone to confession to Father Ambrosi, Alberto Ruiz "heard from inside: 'You shall become a priest.'" He doesn't know how to explain the voice or how it was expressed. "All I know is that during confession I knew I would become a priest in that Cursillo at the age of thirty-three, and I proceeded."

The path to a priestly ordination can be circuitous indeed. For sure it isn't always direct and when it curves, it may do so in a most sweeping fashion. How else can Alberto Ruiz's journey be described?

He obtained a Master's Degree in International Marketing Business Networks and then pursued this course by working for corporations internationally for almost nine years, the most recent time having been spent in Brazil. He felt that in life, he has been significantly led by women and people who are Spanish. This feeling was borne out by the gift to him of a book from his sister who was a Nun at the time and by the subject of that book, namely St. Therese of Avila, a Spanish Nun. When Father Ruiz reflects back on Saint Therese, he says he fell in love with her and "Fell in love with her idea of how to talk back to God." Greatly influenced by this saint who is a Doctor of the Church, he planned to leave

Brazil. But his day of choice for departure was not possible and it was apparently on an insignificant day in 1977 that he was actually able to leave. That day, however was far from insignificant as it was December the eighth, the Feast of The Immaculate Conception, the glorious feast of Mary, the Mother of God. Further emphasis would be put on this day when it would became the actual date of Alberto's ordination to the priesthood seven years later as a Claretian, a Missionary Son of The Immaculate Heart of Mary.

When Alberto became a Novice, he was sent to Berkley, California for his first year of Theology. For the second year in the Novitiate he found himself in Los Angeles right next to the Claretian Provincial House where Father Aloysius resided. This was a convenient location for Alberto to see Father often to attend his Masses and to pray the Rosary. But this acquaintance didn't happen immediately for Alberto because his initial attitude toward Father was one of fear and apprehension. He would hear stories about Father Aloysius that would elicit his admiration; yet he wondered whether these events could really be true. Proximity and the passage of time would help to bolster Alberto's courage and eventually he was able to go to Father for Confession. Here he saw the Grace of God ministered by this priest with great compassion. This virtue of compassion which Father Aloysius possessed touched his heart so deeply that it became a major goal for his own future ministry. He recalls the comforting words spoken to him in the confessional when the reply given by Father Aloysius was the simple encouraging words in addressing him as: "My son;" and the consoling advice for him to: "Try harder." At one time, he remembers telling Father: "You know, I'm scared of you." Again, with a big accent, comforting words were given: "No, no, no, my son, you should never fear, you don't have to be scared of me."

One day, as Alberto walked into the Chapel, he was a bit surprised to see Father Aloysius there on his knees praying before the statue of the Blessed Mother. Always aware of Father's sanctity and spiritual gifts, Alberto again found himself apprehensive, knowing that Father was able to read hearts. He didn't want to walk out because he thought he could be heard and that would surely give away his presence. Wanting to hide, Alberto went over to the right hand side before the tabernacle, covered his face and tried to pray. He hoped that Father would either leave the Chapel or at least not come over by him. He was afraid that Father would come over. Sure enough, Father stood up and walked over to Alberto and told him what he was thinking and after blessing him, Father told him of some future event. True to this prediction, the event came to pass later after Father's death. Then, when Father left the Chapel, Alberto began to wonder if all of this had really happened. "Did I make it up? Am I foolish to go say this to someone. And if I do, does that mean I am privileged?" He was now the victim of mixed emotions and concerns. He never related these events until years later.

The humanness of Father Aloysius again became apparent when on a trip to the Placita in Los Angeles for adoration, Father expressed his hopes for Ronald Reagan to win the presidential election whereas others who were nearby disagreed with his choice. Alberto was impressed with this humanness to be able to discuss and argue about current affairs. On this same trip, with the ability to shift his thought to spiritual matters, Father told those who were with him: "When I die, I'm going to come back for all of you." These words caught Alberto's attention because they were the same type of words that had been used by St. Therese of Lisieux.

If Father Aloysius was ever to be embarrassed or humiliated he surely had the opportunity one time when he fell in the shower and could not get up without assistance. It was particularly at this time during our interview that Father Alberto spoke so very dearly about Father Aloysius and related how he and three or more of the other Novices really loved him. It was the Novices who helped Father get up without creating any alarm in the house because they concluded that Father would not want anyone to know about the accident and thus necessitate a trip to the hospital.

Alberto became familiar with the weekly gatherings in the Provincial House for Benediction and blessings. On these occasions, giving deference to the crowd of people present, he thought it would be best to wait under last to receive Father's blessing; so this was his practice. But one time, he waited too long because when it became his turn, he thought that "Father went into an ecstasy." This was not actually verified since he had been very tired at the time and he was possibly exhausted. Not only did he bless people after the weekly Novenas but actually he did so at any time that he was requested; day or night made no difference. Even when he was quite ill he never withheld a blessing if it were at all possible.

The unique aroma which others had noticed when Father was present, was also evident to Alberto and Larry

Gerkin when they were Novices. The closest identification that Alberto can assign to this aroma is that of being like roses.

When he was ordained as a Claretian, Father Alberto felt that the Blessed Mother had a firm hold on his life. His love for his Claretian Order deepened when he was sent to the Missions in Africa where he was soon to be left alone when the fellow members of his community got sick and had to leave. His loneliness grew during the nine month period that he served by himself. This experience was a great opportunity to learn the value of community life.

When reviewing his life, Father Alberto happily announces that October 12, 1945 was the date of his birth. This is a Marian day in Brazil called the Day of the Child and in Spain it is significant because it is the Feast of Our Lady of Pilar. He left us with the remembrance of a phrase that had been given to him. On his wallboard it said: "Coincidence is when God works a miracle and decides to remain anonymous."

Chapter Seventeen

<u>Lisa Tobias and Melba Esparza</u>

Lisa Tobias and her mother, Melba Esparza met with us in their San Diego home on March 5, 1991 while Lisa's ten month old daughter Katrina sat on her mother's lap. On many occasions, Father Aloysius had gone to San Diego where he had a monthly meeting of his Guild. There would be spiritual exercises, a talk by Father and a potluck meal for all. These Guilds of his were very special groups of lay people formed for the advancement of spirituality and they also provided camaraderie among the friends of Father. This particular San Diego Guild was formed mostly of those people who had gone on the 1968 European Pilgrimage with Father.

The tour began in Portugal and encompassed Spain France and Italy with their numerous shrines and other holy places.The visit that was scheduled for Foggia, Italy to see Padre Pio, unfortunately was not meant to be. Two days before the date for departure for Foggia, the group received word of Padre Pio's death. And another planned visit to a stigmatist, Mother Esperanza, was in jeopardy due to a confusion in schedule. Fortunately this latter event was successful nevertheless, since Mother Esperanza graciously received the group by providing time in her busy schedule. At the time of this visit, Melba and her husband Al were particularly consoled by this holy nun. Shortly before the tour had begun, Al's mother had died and this situation now lingered in his thoughts as I will relate.

Since the time available to be with Mother Esperanza was so tight, the tour group was told not to talk to her. They should just bring their things and she will hold them in her hand and Father Aloysius would bless them. But Al was too intent, and as Melba tells it: "My husband couldn't contain himself, he just blurted out: 'My Mother!' Immediately he received his consolation when Mother Esperanza responded: "She's in heaven."

As in past interviews, it seemed to be a very similar description that would be given when one was asked to tell about the blessing which Father Aloysius gave to them. Melba says that: "He'd hold your head and you just really felt blessed after he was finished. It would take him quite a while...you could almost feel it going right through you." When asked if she noticed anything else different about Father Aloysius, she said: "Very, very holy; and when you were with him, especially at a time like this when he blessed you, you just felt that you were very close to God." When Lisa sought to describe her blessing by Father she said: "Father Aloysius would put his hands on your head and it was as though he could read your heart." Upon receiving one of these blessings in Los Angeles, Lisa had asked Father to pray for her grandmother who was quite ill and it was this grandmother that at a later date would be declared to be in heaven.

Now another serious illness beset the Esparza family: Al, who was Melba's husband and Lisa's father was critically ill in Mercy Hospital in San Diego. One day in September of 1981, Lisa and her husband were hurrying to the hospital to see Al. They parked their car and worked their way through the construction area outside.

But before they crossed the street, Lisa said: "I happened to look up and out from the hospital door came Father Aloysius." Then she said to her husband: "That's Father Aloysius, he's gone to see Daddy." Now, Melba reminded Lisa of the additional words that she had spoken: "Daddy must really be bad if they called for Father Aloysius."

After spotting Father Aloysius across the street, coming out of the hospital, Lisa saw him proceeding down the street -----but due to construction there was nowhere for him to go. Lisa said: "We were crossing the street, and I turned to look; he was gone. There was nobody there." Lisa was not surprised to see Father Aloysius but she was surprised when he was no longer visible. And Lisa continued: "I never thought anything of it until later when I had said (to someone): "Father Aloysius was here, and they said: 'Don't be ridiculous, Father's been dead.' And I didn't know that he had died; I had no idea."

At this point, Lisa stuck firmly to her story even after we confronted her with the fact that Father had died in April of 1981, and her view of Father had been on the first or second of September in 1981; five months after his death. She insisted that she had seen Father with a slight smile and a gentleness that just emanated; "just kind of a glow." She didn't talk to him from across the street but she certainly knew who he was. Her husband also saw Father even though he didn't know who he was because they had never met. He just knew that he saw a priest.

Then, Lisa arrived at her father's bedside but she hadn't had a chance to talk to him because he was not "really conscious." Heretofore, she used to talk to him and get a response in writing, but not this time. It is definite then that Father Aloysius had the opportunity to see Al before he died. In fact, Al lingered until September 11th before he died.

To firmly establish the creditability of this after death appearance of Father Aloysius, I questioned Lisa repeatedly by asking how he was dressed and how many times had she seen him before and even how old was Lisa at the time. He "looked like he always looked, he was dressed in black, with a jacket and pants and with the collar," as she stated; and at this time, Lisa was about 26 years old. She had seen Father Aloysius on several occasions but particularly she gave the impression of her ability to identify Father when she told of a wedding where she had been the maid of honor: "It was in the small chapel down at St. Charles and it was very open, very small and all of us were so fortunate to be right there on the altar with Father. You could see every bit of him, every part of him, watching how he would go through the ceremony."

Father Aloysius and Al Esparza were both Basque and Al was younger by about ten years. Al spoke only a few words of the Basque language but like Father, he spoke Spanish fluently. They both died in 1981.

Chapter Eighteen

Ruben and Lorraine De Lira

Once again at the home of Melba Esparza on March 5, 1981, Dr. Ruben De Lira and his wife Lorraine graciously agreed to be interviewed while we were in San Diego. They too had been on the European Pilgrimage of 1968 with Father Aloysius. And like other interviewees, they were most enthusiastic in their responses. Lorraine's animation at this time was quite effective as a means of expression. Her actions endowed authenticity to her words. Her husband Ruben, although not equally animated, nevertheless was not wanting in his conviction. Their two Pilgrimages with Father to Europe in 1968 and 1970 were certainly highlights of their life and remained in their memory even to the minutest detail. They were filled, in fact they were overloaded with great examples of spirituality and spectacles of enormous interest. People have often spoken of these tours as being very taxing physically and most rewarding spiritually because of the many graces received. To witness Father's participation and exuberance in all of the aspects was an absolute delight and frequently left the participants speechless. For this interview, the earlier Pilgrimage was the one that was mostly discussed. The spirit of such a journey was established early in the trip by their recitation of the Holy Rosary which continued almost incessantly during the flight across the ocean. Even when weariness prevailed during the flight when heads were nodding to sleep, the Rosary continued for those who could participate. Nor did this devotion stop during the bus segments of the tour.

Acquaintance with Father Aloysius for Ruben and Lorraine began probably in the early sixties when Father would journey to San Diego with the Blue Army and he began to form a lay religious society called the Lay Apostolate of Mary Brotherhood (LAMB). The Saturday night agenda for this group was followed by Sunday morning Mass which Father celebrated. From the very beginning of this relationship with Father, it was evident that "He was not like a normal ordinary priest;" says Lorraine. Ruben says he noticed the great spirituality of Father because "He was very devout and conscious about the holy places and the presence of God in the church." Memorable too, were the blessings which Father imparted with his hands cupping their heads. As he continued with his impressions, he spoke of Father's very profound veneration of the Holy Eucharist: "Because when he used to elevate the host during Mass, he used to do it with such a reverence and such a profound respect that he used to take a very long time in elevating the Host and stay with it up for quite some time and he would look up to heaven." It was as though he could see up through the roof and into the sky.

Lorraine recounted an episode from the past as she told of Leonard Greenwall, a saintly man in San Diego who was very active in his zeal for the Church and for Father Aloysius. Through Father, this man had been cured of a number of severe ailments such as very arthritic knees. Apparently, Leonard had not requested any of these cures but they had been the result of Father's diligence in noticing Leonard's condition. On one occasion, Leonard decided to give three rosaries to Ruben and Lorraine. There was one for each of them and one for them to give away. Lorraine cherished her blue rosary while Ruben, appreciative of his green gift, had reservations about the blessings which Leonard had attributed to them. The story which Leonard told was that Sister Rita, an Augustinian cloistered nun in Northern Italy had given several rosaries to a Mr. Joseph Jasper of Teagod, Oregon and then they had been passed on to Leonard. These rosaries were not made by the Sisters in that convent but were given to the Sisters and were supposed to have been blessed by Our Lord, the Blessed Mother and Padre Pio. Not only was this an outstanding claim to have been made, but Sister Rita herself was a most unusual nun. As a child, she was favored to pray with the Infant Jesus and she received the stigmata at the age of fourteen and a half years and entered the convent at the age of about nineteen. Shortly after entering the convent, she began a life of great austerity; she neither ate nor slept. Now, at the age of forty-eight, it is quite obvious that she is a chosen soul.

The beginning of the story really goes back to a Marilla Phillips of San Francisco who while visiting Italy in about 1958 came across a convent that was destitute. In her desire to help these Sisters, Marilla became aware of Sister Rita and of her recital of the fifteen decades of the Rosary which she would say in the presence of Our Lord, The Blessed Mother and Padre Pio. Marilla then suggested to the Reverend Mother that rosaries could be the source of solicitation for donations for the convent and its twenty-four Sisters who were now in residence. Then too, these rosaries could be a source of spiritual assistance to those who would be the recipients of them. It was at this time then, that the Sisters decided to buy the rosaries outside of the convent and then present them to others for donations. And they were assured that The Blessed Mother held each rosary in her hand. It is easy to understand then that this convent became the source of many rosaries.

The following information that was read by Lorraine is a continuation of a portion of the text from the lengthy pamphlet that had accompanied the rosaries:

"Since Sister has not slept or eaten since shortly after entering the convent, except the Holy Eucharist, she is a victim soul who prays and suffers for the salvation of other souls. Early each morning, Padre Pio, The Blessed Virgin, and most often, Our Lord comes to her cell to pray the Rosary; fifteen decades for the salvation of souls. At the conclusion of the fifteen decades, the rosaries which have been purchased outside of the convent, are brought into Sister's cell, are then blessed by Padre Pio, The Blessed Virgin and Our Lord. It is then that The Blessed Virgin holds these rosaries in her hand and runs her fingers over the beads. If this occurs on a day when Our Lord does not appear, they are left on the table in Sister Rita's room until (He) does come. Hence, all rosaries have His blessing. The reason that nobody has heard of Sister Rita is because it is the wish of Our Lord that there be nothing published about her until after her death lest she be scrutinized, tested and derided as has happened in the past to Theresa Neumann, Padre Pio and others….. There would be many curiosity seekers who would interrupt the serenity of the convent and disturb the primary purpose of the life of Sister Rita which is indeed that of a victim soul. The side effect if you wish, are these precious rosaries. If you will find many who are not aware nor do they understand the spiritual and mystic life of the Church, these are the same types to leave alone. And if anyone doubts the truthfulness as to the origin of these rosaries, they are better off to take the money they would have donated for the rosaries and go buy themselves a good meal. These rosaries are meant to be used; not as a collector's item to be thrown in the corner of some drawer."

Lorraine provided the reason for reading such a lengthy pamphlet when she proceeded in her discussion: ..."I assume it was in the early sixties, sixty-three or sixty-four that we got these from Leonard Greenwall. I don't even think Leonard took a donation from us; he just wanted to give them to us......We read it and I accepted it, but Thomas, over here (pointing to her husband, Ruben) ....Thomas had doubts; he didn't know. He loved the rosary; it was a very beautiful rosary but he had doubts to the validity of these rosaries. He was going to write Padre Pio. And I believe he had the letter composed and written when Padre Pio died."

Discussion of the Pilgrimage then continued as Lorraine tried to describe the many beautiful sights they had visited and how wonderful it was to be with Father Aloysius: "Each Pilgrimage stop we made was more magnificent. The first stop would have been enough for me and surely it would be understandable if that were the case." Lorraine thought back to the time of landing in Portugal and preparation for their visit to Fatima. As they were leaving the airport to make this drive, she approached Father Aloysius to discuss the miracle of the Bleeding Host at Santarém. It didn't take long for Father to decide that such a venue would be most desirable before proceeding to Fatima. How wonderful it was to have this miraculous location lie right in their path just a half hour drive from Fatima. Father immediately located the church and had the rector open it for the pilgrims. When Father related the whole history behind this Bleeding Host, he held the reliquary in the cradle of his arm as though he were holding the Christ Child. As Lorraine stepped up to venerate the Host, she felt that Father had an ongoing vision of this Child in his arms.

Throughout the pilgrimages, the participants were able to learn much about the Saints whose shrines were visited. For example, noteworthy attention was given to such saints as St. Catherine Labouré, St. Bernadette Soubirous and St. Rita Cascia.

Some people just wanted to hover around Father Aloysius all the time; we didn't, we just kind of stayed back and absorbed everything. And it was a great blessing just doing that. Until one day, I believe it was Vern Hupka, came to us and he said that Father Aloysius had come to him and said that he had not had an opportunity to get close to Ruben and me on this whole Pilgrimage and at some time he would like to sit (with them and have dinner.) We said that we would be delighted but we were not pushing ourselves on him. He had the freedom to choose with whom he wanted to eat and to go his own way and we were just like onlookers. So, Vern Hupka arranged a table for five of us. There were two couples, the four of us and Father Aloysius." At this point, Lorraine went to great length to depict the table setting for themselves with Father and the other people who were named Sampson. She said: "I can recall it with a great deal of detail. I was just so floored and flustered to be sitting next to someone so holy that my heart started going a little bit. But Ruben never goes through those flusters that I go through. So the first thing he does as we sit down, he reaches into his pocket and pulls out (the rosary) and says: 'Father, I want to ask you something. I want to know if this is true. I was told that The Blessed Mother, Padre Pio, Our Lord and a Sister who has the stigmata prayed with these rosaries or touched these rosaries. And I want to know if this is authentic.'" Ruben then added his emphasis by saying: "I wanted to find out if the story was correct.....all these could be distorted...I wanted to find out if that was correct." Lorraine then added her own recollection of Ruben's conversation with: "I think he said I just want to know if it is true because I don't want to say something; I don't want to read something that is not the truth.....he put his hands right in Father's." It was here that Lorraine began a lengthy, animated portrayal of Father Aloysius. "Father's hand just cupped this rosary with a little cross like this.....and he looked at these rosaries very lovingly and he was sort of sitting there like this and he went kind of like this, just leaned over and....I was sitting here, I could see. I was sitting next to a man that was just a shell! I just sort of felt his spirit leave. It just left.....and he was just...he looked like a crumpled....I don't think the table was holding him up because his head wasn't down, but he's sort of a round rotund man, you know.....his head rest on his shoulder and he kept holding this.......he was slumped over. His arm was on the table resting. He still had the rosary in his hand with the crucifix up like this and he was just kind of crumpled over....my sitting at this end of the table, I had the full view. Ruben and Mr. Sampson probably only saw the top of his head and his back. I don't know what Mrs. Sampson saw. But anyway, he was like this to me for

111

quite some time......I thought....as a matter of fact, I don't remember eating much that day, I was so in awe over the whole experience. But anyway, he just stayed this way and then I felt him come back and somehow or other he felt his spirit....I don't know if you could call it a force, but you felt this come back into his body. And he picked up his hand, he looked at this and he just went like this (kissing the rosary). And he opened his hand and he held it back to Ruben and he said: 'We must go there.'"

Due to the tight schedule that was pursued, there was not sufficient time for the group to journey to see Sister Rita. Lorraine's final description was: "...Such a tight schedule that we were on. Every day was filled to the hilt and we were going many hours....a rather exhausting trip. No, we did not make it (to see Sister Rita), but to me that answered it, I felt this was bilocation; this is my own interpretation because I think this man was....I can't say he was dead, I don't know that much about it but I just know I was sitting next to a shell. It was a shell! I don't remember any breathing. His spirit left him"

Later in the tour, they visited Mother Esperanza as Melba Esparza had related. And now Lorraine repeated the episode with Mother Esperanza that Melba had related wherein Mother stated that Al Esparza's mother was now in heaven.

After visiting Mother Esperanza and having received her blessing, the group proceeded to the church where Father Aloysius said Mass. In her effort to describe the scene at Mass, Lorraine again became very animated: "It was a very beautiful Mass; I shall never forget it, I was so taken back by Father, how he interacted while he was saying Mass. You often felt he was with the saints; it was just a real experience. And it was during this time that I saw him at the elevation, I believe it was when he lifted up the chalice, I just kept seeing him, I just kept seeing him going up. And I was trying to look. I wanted to verify if what I was seeing. Was his feet off the ground? I thought, if his feet are off the ground, then I know I'm not hallucinating or I'm not seeing things. I just kept seeing him go. And I couldn't see, here was an obstruction. I don't know if it was people's heads or something from the altar. I could not see his feet. After the Mass was over, we were all so touched and I remember I had made some comment to her (Katherine Morrow). I said, you know, I just felt that I saw Father Aloysius elevate, go up; and she said: 'I saw the same thing. He did, he did! He went up.' I thought, well, I was seeing right. And she said: 'Oh, yes.'" And Lorraine thinks that Katherine may know of other people who saw it. Then, Lorraine looked at Ruben and said: "I asked Rubin and he said he didn't." So, I asked: "He was at the Mass with you?" Lorraine's response was: "Yes, he was right next to me." I continued then with: "Ruben was there and he didn't see it. Mary was there and she didn't see it. Right, Mary?" When Mary assured me that she didn't see it either, Lorraine turned to Melba who stated that neither she nor her husband, Al had seen it. Lorraine's final comment was: "I was right there. When I talked to Katherine, and I felt Katherine was a very solid person, and I thought she called the shots the way she saw 'em so…Katherine saw it. She said: 'I saw it and I'm going to stick by my guns.'" A subsequent interview which we had with Katherine Morrow failed to provide conclusive proof of this event.

During the 1960's, several apparitions of The Blessed Mother have been said to have occurred in Garabandal, Spain. I personally experienced the interest that Father Aloysius had in these events. When I review the video interviews which I made and recall my own conversations with Father about these reports from Garabandal, I see a continual attitude and proclamation by him of total conformity with Church decrees. He neither advocated nor condemned these occurrences. Rather, very emphatically he taught us that possible veracity could be declared by the Church alone. He himself would not give approval of apparitions nor would he visit the locale when such visits were not allowed.

A Pilgrimage experience with Father Aloysius is so impressive that it seems to last forever. This fact was borne out by Dr. DeLira's recounting of church visits: "Just look at Father Aloysius when you go in a church and he sees a statue of The Blessed Virgin Mary. As he approaches a statue, it is as if it is alive; as if she's speaking to him. And he always would touch the statue very gently....wasn't like he was touching a piece of wood or plaster, or whatever the statue would be made of. It was always as if it were living." Such tenderness by Father was displayed also in the city of Carcassonne, France's famous medieval walled city. While waiting a long period of time for a meal to be served in a local restaurant where there was a prominent statue of The Child Jesus, it was obvious that the owner: "had a tremendous devotion to the Child Jesus, and while we were waiting, Father Aloysius watched this statue closely and was venerating (it) with the same tender approach, and the same reverence. He was talking, praying, and spent the most part of the time in conversation and praying with The Child Jesus and with the same tenderness that he used to show to The Virgin Mother too."

A period of profound meditation by Father was not unusual as was the case when Lorraine was preparing a meal one time and Father with his eyes closed seemed to be in prayer. Whether it was prayer, meditation, or sleep, was the problem that the DeLiras had to determine. After some period of time, the meal was now ready to be served but Father was still very quiet; many times moving his head. Ruben and Lorraine were very reluctant to disturb Father as the dinner was getting cold. Finally, deciding to take action, they approached Father: "Father, dinner is ready." "I'll be there; I'll be there" he responded and then went back into his meditative state. With another entreaty to Father, pleading the problem of a cold meal, he finally got up and they went to eat. As Ruben said: "Typical of him, time for him didn't exist." Nor did time seem to exist when the Pilgrimage was pursuing their schedule. Michael Murphy who was conducting the schedule was the one to prod Father to move on. "....or his talks used to take a long time; a very long time, and some time the people started to get anxious. Some of these talks at night used to go to eleven or even eleven thirty and people were already falling asleep."

Who among us can lead a perfect life and thus be exempt from all imperfection. We would be remiss were we to portray Father Aloysius in such a light. Like all of us, he had his imperfections. There is the necessity to portray him as a human being in possession of a truly human nature. He cannot be pictured as one whose level of virtue is unattainable. Though we may never reach this level, we still must know that it is not an impossible goal. Scripture itself tells us of the justified anger which Our Lord Himself displayed at the money changers in the temple. We can well imagine that Jesus must have raised His voice to some degree when necessary in order to convey His message.

On occasion, Father Aloysius displayed righteous indignation for the purpose of achieving what is in accordance with his plans. There was an incident on one of the Pilgrimages when some of the people were listening to Spanish music which was decent and enjoyable. Yet at this time, Father displayed his Basque temperament when he demanded that this music be turned off. There was no wrong being done, but there was an air of revelry which Father deemed inappropriate at that moment. Apparently, though it was innocent, it must have disturbed the spiritual tenor of the moment.

When the time came for all of the members of the tour to be introduced to Mother Esperanza in Cova Valencia, Portugal, there was an ardent desire of Father Aloysius to have his Pilgrims be received individually by Mother. This wish of Father was not easy to attain because the priest who was in charge had set up some type of protection for Mother to safely deal with the multitude of people. In fact, the entire visit was in jeopardy due to the time constraints which the crowds had put upon this holy nun. Apparently, this audience with Mother was one of the major goals of the entire trip. It was only by a rigorous display of his anxiety and the fact that he was visibly upset that he was granted the time necessary for his party to be received by this nun who had been held in such high esteem by Father Aloysius. Lorraine said that a story told by Father Aloysius about that locale dealt with the search for water which seemed to be definitely out of the question geologically. After fruitless digging and digging, the pursuit went on at the urging from Mother Esperanza to go another two hundred feet. Sure enough, they hit it then. Because of Mother Esperanza's prayers, an immense amount of water came up from this well.

When our interview was supposedly completed, Lorraine said she wanted to provide some further information to add to that which had been given by Lisa Esparza regarding the post death appearance by Father Aloysius to Al Esparza who was dying in Mercy Hospital in San Diego. When Melba had told Lorraine about Father's visit to Al in the hospital, Lorraine was very impressed because she knew that God had given many gifts to Father and she wanted to confirm this visit as being an actual occurrence. When Lorraine saw Al immobilized with so many tubes to his body in the Intensive Care unit of the hospital, he seemed to her to resemble the crucified Christ with his arms extended. Lorraine said: "When we went in to see him (Al) in the Intensive Care, Ruben was going to ask him in Spanish if Father Aloysius was here to see him. And we stood there and he recognized both of us. And I think Ruben asked him in Spanish and I asked him in English; I said: 'Al, was Father Aloysius here to see you?' And he went.....(Lorraine, at this time made a sudden thrust backward in her chair, with her arms outstretched in order to imitate Al's reaction to the question.) Just at the name of Father Aloysius, he gave.......but then the nurse loused it up. I was so aggravated with those.....There was this nurse that was giving attention, and she said: 'Oh, there was nobody here to see him. Nobody gets in here to see him....but nobody gets in here to see him, you know.'" And Lorraine continued: "We wondered what he had to say, but just at the name of Father Aloysius we got the reaction. Now, as I say, I was very upset because I thought the nurse blew it for us. And then of course, his awake time was not.....he would go on, and he never came back after that......after that he never came back." Al Esparza and Father Aloysius Ellacuria, two Basque friends, had kept their visit to themselves.

Chapter Nineteen

Father Don Lavelle, C.M.F.

It was always important when choosing people to be interviewed that we made certain to select people from a variety of sources. We wanted to include as many different views and as many different observations and opinions as possible. Sometimes, we were able to accurately document events from a first person stand point whereas at other times such precision was not possible. Such was the case with the visit that we made to Father Don Lavelle, C.M.F. who was able to provide fascinating accounts in the life of Father Aloysius but because of the passage of time, he was not able to recall some names and dates. Even in cases like this, every bit of the history of Father Aloysius is valuable and fits into the overall mosaic of his life.

Father Don Lavelle was born in 1921 in Chicago where he remained until he was nine years old. At the age of fourteen, he entered the Claretian Seminary in Walnut California. Located near the city of Pomona, this Seminary was called Silver Peak. After spending four years there he then entered the Novitiate at Dominguez in Compton, California. Sometime later, in order to attain accelerated courses during the war time era, he was sent to Washington, D.C. When the war ended, he returned to Dominguez. This is where Father Aloysius was the Prefect for a good number of years. Another role that Father Aloysius also filled for some time at the Seminary was that of Novice Master. Apparently he was well suited for these assignments because he had previously been the Prefect and the Rector of the Minor Seminary in Momence, Illinois.

Father Lavelle was at the Dominguez Seminary in Compton, California on February 8, 1991 for this interview. Of particular interest at this time was the need to have him identify numerous photographs which had been accumulated and showed the era of Father Aloysius' life that was spent in Illinois as well as the years which he spent at Dominguez Seminary.

Repeatedly during interviews, as was the case now with Father Lavelle, emphasis was given to the comments which people made to describe the aura of holiness that was so obvious when they were in the presence of Father Aloysius. Although they didn't all describe it as such, they were visibly moved by their belief that he lived in the presence of Almighty God.

Father Lavelle said: "I am happy to help in this drive in any way that I can because I feel that Father Aloysius was a very good priest and I think he was a very holy man. But he was a controversial figure, as most well known people are. Even some of our great leaders in the Church today are loved and some are (not). One I could mention is Cardinal Ratzinger who I think the world of. He is well thought of by many people and detested by others: I suppose mainly by those who are uncomfortable with his Theology: the Theology of the Church for the last two thousand years."

Father Lavelle continues by saying: "Father Aloysius is also well known by many people. Some did not like him; some liked him very much, some loved him. Some thought that he was maybe too extreme in some of his ideas or that he did not understand the American psyche of young people because he was in charge of Seminarians.

I have no personal experiences of anything that you would call supernatural: visions or locutions, or things that might have happened in his life. One incident I could tell you, but (there is) no way of verifying this because I don't remember names and I don't remember the exact time of this happening. But, a good number of years back, when I was stationed in Chicago, my cousin's husband passed away. My cousin was Gertrude Riley, and her husband was Charles. They had three boys: two were Seminarians at Mundelein. One of them got as far as his last year in Theology and had to drop out because of problems of his health. Another son decided that God was not calling him to the priesthood, but to married life. He dropped out. Now he had a lot of friends that were priests. So, at the funeral of their father, many priests came for the funeral. And while I was talking in the corner of the funeral parlor in Chicago, one priest came in and said: 'Which one of you is a Claretian?' I said: 'I am, Father.' "

This priest called Father Lavelle over in the corner, a large private area. He said that he had just gotten back from Los Angeles, California where he had been on vacation to visit various scenic places. Through strange circumstances and surely not his own desire, the first place that he happened to visit was the Claretian

Provincial House because he was told that there was someone special there. Just dropping in to say hello, he met Father Aloysius. As Father Aloysius came down the hallway and entered the parlor, he seemed to be rapt in prayer. His hands were almost always folded and his eyes were down. After the usual courteous greetings, Father told this priest that he was so happy for the visit and he knew that he was a good priest. In similar words, he said: "I know you've had problems in your life;" and then began to relate event after event that this priest had encountered. The priest was absolutely dumbfounded as he was now practically hearing a recount of his past life. There were pitfalls, ups and downs, which had never been related. Then Father Aloysius continued saying somewhat: "But Father, I know now that you're trying to be a good priest;" citing numerous examples of his actions. Similarly, Father Aloysius let him know that "God is going to bless you and God is Blessing you for this; continue what you are doing." Such an encounter which this priest had with Father Aloysius, left him awestruck and so obviously grateful that he felt compelled to tell his story to another Claretian priest, Father Don Lavelle.

Again, Fr. Lavelle remembers when he was a student at Dominguez Seminary during the 1940s and Father Aloysius was the Prefect who was immediately in charge: the one who guided the Seminarians. These Seminarians, since they were students, were not sup-posed to mix with the Community---with the professors, the teachers, or the priests, unless there was some official business. If there was such business to be discussed, it had to be arranged through the Prefect who in turn would schedule to meet in the parlor. One day, Seminarian

Gerard Shawn was walking up the front road and he stopped to talk to some priest. Later, when Gerard was about to enter the Study Hall, he had to pass the Prefect's Office where the door happened to be open. Father Aloysius said: "Mister Shawn, come here." So, Gerard went in and sat down. Father then said: "Do you realize that you are not allowed to talk to other members of the Community without permission and you were breaking that rule. And you were also complaining about things. You were talking about this and this......" In this recounting, Gerald (now Monsignor Gerald Shawn) said to Father Lavelle: "How in the world did he know that I was talking with him. Maybe he could run out quick, look and run back in again. But I don't think he did. But not only that, how would he know that I was talking about this and that? It kind of mystified me."

Father Lavelle also recalled the great esteem that his own sister and so many other of her friends in San Pedro had for Father Aloysius. Not only was he a holy man but he was the source of great spiritual advice for them.

Chapter Twenty

Lorraine and Rudy Vega with Esther de la Torre

Our travels brought us to Santa Ana, California on August 10, 2000 to see Esther, Rudy and Lorraine. After a brief and pleasant chat with Rudy, we turned our attention to Lorraine and her mother Esther.

Esther was the motivation for a relationship with Father Aloysius. In the early seventies when she was sick, she was told that there was a priest in Los Angeles who could help her. She was continually sick and was ailing particularly at this time with a virus. She followed through with the advice that was given and visited Father Aloysius. Most probably she recovered from her malady because she never spoke about it again. Instead, she turned her full attention to her grandson Stephen who was the principal subject of our visit.

Stephen was a very sick baby from the time of his birth. For the first two months of his life, they struggled with his need for constant attention. He had been in and out of the hospital from the first day. The baby couldn't swallow properly and his nursing episodes were followed by projectile vomiting. The only recourse to counter this problem was to maintain a strict positional regimen after every feeding. He could not be placed in a prone position. He would first be placed in an infant seat for twenty minutes and then be taken down and gently handled while maintaining an upright attitude. Even with the twenty four hour attention and vigilant care, Stephen was facing a tremendous battle. When he was almost two months old and very much underweight, Father blessed him. Lorraine cherishes the picture that she displayed. It shows Father holding the baby right after he had blessed him and stated that he would be well and become big and strong. Such a statement was much welcomed by Lorraine because she had received a dire prognosis from her pediatrician: "The muscle into his stomach was not developed. It would take five to seven years before it would fully develop." It was also believed that the child had heart murmurs. Because of prior scheduling, Lorraine proceeded with the EKG procedure to be done. It was a nun who performed the test and it so happened that she knew Father Aloysius. Esther proclaimed to this nun: "We just came from Father Aloysius, he's healed. There's nothing wrong with him." The veracity of this statement was proven in subsequent visits to Father. At Father's request, Lorraine brought Stephen back to see Father every day for a week. At each visit, Father would inquire: "Is he all right?" Lorraine's response was always the same: "He's eating and he is fine." hen the time came for Father to baptize the baby, it was unfortunate that Father became sick and was unable to do so.

At the time of this interview, Stephen was twenty-four years old and stood six feet tall. Lorraine estimated his weight to be about 225 pounds. We didn't get to see him because he had just left the house before we arrived.

It is never surprising, but rather expected to see the peripheral fruits which are brought about through the healings that are effected through the ministry of Father

Aloysius. Lorraine was ready to admit that initially she did not believe in this healing. Here is how she put it: "I wasn't really a strong Catholic at the time. I had gone to different churches in my years during high school and college." When God's Grace took hold of her, she "became very close to Father Aloysius." In these very words, Lorraine epitomized the spiritual conversion that has taken place in so many hearts.

In numerous instances, the Faith may have been implanted but lay somewhat dormant or nebulous. Then, with the imparting of Father's blessing, souls have become convicted, fervent and resolute. From tepidity there arises vigor and commitment to this newborn conversion. This transformation has been exhibited in numerous personal conversations but it rings out so strongly in the people with whom I have been privileged to interview.

Chapter Twenty-One

<u>Jim Buehner</u>

Every interview seemed to tell a story from a different angle and that was the beauty of having such a diverse group of people with which to work. Sometimes miracles stood out more glaringly, sometimes simple human occurrences were highlighted. In any case, the personal sanctity of Father Aloysius was always clearly evident and as such it became the main focus of our attention. The story which was told by Jim Buehner definitely emphasized this situation. It presents miracles and poignant human events but it resounds through most emphatically with the peace, the beauty and the attraction which springs forth from the indwelling of the Holy Spirit.

Jim, who is now deceased, was a very good friend of mine and we collaborated on various projects. Jim was a kindred spirit in apologetics and in science. His limited egress was due to emphysema but his determination was never diminished. He was a scientist, a chemist and an author. Foremost however, he was an outstanding Catholic layman. He was born in Waterloo, Iowa in 1924, the son of a railroader and one of five children. Having completed high school in1941, he soon moved to San Diego, California. It wasn't long before the outbreak of World War II and then in early 1943 he volunteered for the Air Force where he served as an aerial engineer on B24 bombers. When he had completed 39 missions and received his discharge, he returned to his native State and on the last day of 1945, he married Mary Elizabeth

Heckart who was an established Country and Western singer on the Des Moines radio station, WHO. Jim matriculated into Drake University where he received his degree in Chemistry. Then later in 1951, he and Mary moved to Torrance, California where their family grew to include three sons and four daughters. During this period, hard times beset the family as Jim was plagued by health and employment problems. But interestingly, Jim relates this era as an indication that "God works in strange ways, His wonders to perform."

Jim developed an errant disc in his back and was accepted into the Veteran's Hospital for corrective surgery. After ten days in the hospital, the surgery was scheduled to take place. Such was not to be however, because as he lay on a gurney outside the operating room, a neurosurgeon bent down and said to him in a low voice: "I'm sorry, we can't take you today; you have a slight temperature and we can't take any chance on infection." As a result of this disappointment and the fact that he had already spent so much time in the hospital, Jim was more than ready to return home when the pre-op drugs wore off. In fact, he surely did go home and it was against medical advice that he did so. Thus he didn't qualify for re-admittance to this hospital for another six months. Quite severe pain persisted so often that it caused Jim to seek relief by lying on the floor in various positions. Even though the back pain never stopped, it varied in intensity. Now he began to actively look for a job. His first choice was in his primary field of chemistry. When this effort proved to be unsuccessful and no other opportunities presented themselves, he showed his true spirit when he said: "I asked the Good Lord to direct me to whatever employment He wanted

me to have. And fortuitously, I met Frank and Theresa Gurley, a couple of real estate brokers, whose office was right across from St. James Church, our parish church in Redondo Beach. They hired me as a salesman." The pain in the back persisted but Jim persisted too. One day while in the office with Frank and Theresa, Frank said that he was going to take a woman "down to see this priest." No name was mentioned, but the priest was described as one who had been known to cure people. Frank suggested that Jim go along with him, Theresa and Alice Donovan, the cancer patient, because maybe this priest could do something about his back.

When they arrived at the Claretian Provincial House, they were greeted by Father Aloysius who took them into the chapel for his ardent blessing. Up until this point, Jim had no knowledge of Father whatsoever but he soon got to experience what love and tenderness is like when it is profoundly exhibited. As Jim describes it: "You had to know Father Aloysius and know the warmth of his hands and intensity of prayer to really appreciate what this meant. I felt the warmth but that's all I felt; I did not have any change in the disc problem." On the way out, Father mentioned to Jim, in a low voice: "I feel that The Lord wants you to bear this pain for a while." To this, Jim replied: "I want to do God's Will." And he went on further to say: "If God had willed me to go back and have the operation in six months, I would have accepted that. But Father read a deeper meaning into my words and he said to me something that I have kept a secret and I'm going to continue to keep a secret: about ten words that gave me such reassurance of God's love and renewed confidence and trust in God. The words, and the force behind it, call it The Holy Spirit, were of such intensity that I was almost driven to my knees." After this experience, Jim took Father at his word: "You come and see me whenever you want to." Jim was firmly convinced that Father had read his heart during that first meeting. It was proven to him that Father had the great gift of discerning spirits and of touching hearts. The only other comment that Jim was willing to share about his secret was that it was a very personal prophecy. This introduction to Father Aloysius was a life changing event in that it renewed the faith and trust which Jim already had and added to it in such a way as to influence him for the rest of his life. The first impression which he had in meeting Father was that he was nothing special. He was just an ordinary looking person: "short, Basque background and Basque accent." It didn't take long for this initial impression to disappear when Father began to give his blessings.

Even little things caught the attention of Father Aloysius as at the time when Jim, Mary and their twin girls were visiting him. Father asked Mary if anything was bothering her. She replied: "Father, I have this dry flaky skin patch on my ear and it doesn't matter what I put on it; it doesn't go away. "Father reached over with his thumb and forefinger, touched the ear and rubbed it a little. Then, for whatever reason, he touched it to his lip. After this, Mary had no more problem with her dry flaky skin on her ear lobe.

Jim perceived in Father the ability to sense the presence of his own superior when this man was about to enter, On several occasions, Jim observed Father lapse into silence and look toward the door through which the superior of the house was soon to pass. Jim took this to mean that Father sensed the presence of the superior and since the superior acts in the place of God, Father was showing him that reverence because whatever he might say to Father or not say to Father came right from the mind of God. And Jim enjoyed going to Father for confession although he himself never experienced Father reading his heart as he had heard that he did so in confession with other people. However, when he was outside of the confessional, Jim's heart was no stranger to Father as Jim relates in the following two episodes:

"Mary and I had taken care of the education of a Catholic boy that was living in a home where there was a stepmother and a Catholic father unable to practice the Faith because of a bad marriage. We took Billy into the house and gave him the best on education; we also saw to it that he knew enough of his Faith for his First Holy Communion which he did at the hands of Father John McKenna at our home parish of St. James in Redondo Beach. And then, Billy moved away, but before he did, I went down to see Father one day and I thought on the way down--I just thought to myself--it would be nice if I had some little thing to give Billy that had been blessed by Father Aloysius. I went to confession that day, and immediately after confession , while I was saying my penance, Father left the chapel and came back. And he had a little chain with the rather cheap medal of plastic as I recall, silver, but plastic of St. Anthony Claret. He didn't say a word to me, he just--I don't remember whether he blessed the medal at that time-- he just handed it to me. I took that to mean he had read my thoughts. To kind of substantiate that, I had a similar experience with another boy who was severely retarded. He was the son of a friend of ours from back in Iowa. And I thought that this little fellow does not have any religious education. He couldn't have much because of his retardation and I thought I'd like to have something to at least remind him, and maybe his parents would then give him some instruction at least. So, I was down to see Father that day or another day not long after it, and again, I think I went to confession--I'm not sure--but anyway, Father excused himself long enough to get an ivory beaded, ivory colored beaded string Rosary. Again, another cheapie, but he blessed it and didn't even say who it was for. He knew who it was for.------You kind of guarded your thought around Father, as Mike Murphy, one of his dear friends, who drove him here and there or some other place, found out when he was driving Father along and he thought: 'I wonder if this guy is some sort of a phony.' At which time, Father gave him the elbow in the ribs and said: 'Michael, you're thinking bad thoughts."'

Warmly reminiscent of Father's sweetness, was the occasion one day after Jim's confession when Father took off his Stole, kissed it and put it in the drawer and said to Jim: "Come on now, kneel down and I'll say your penance with you." This love and intimacy which Father showed impacted him profoundly.

At the time of their twenty-fifth wedding anniversary, Jim and Mary were privileged to have Father Aloysius offer the Mass. The celebration at their home after the ceremony included a tiny little daughter from next door who had some kind of hip problem. From time to time, her legs would become un-joined at the hip. She was about six months old and the time was approaching when the doctors thought it would be necessary to perform surgery to correct this condition. The mother who had prepared food for the celebration, was there with the baby. Father Aloysius included all who were present in his blessing. Thus, the little girl whose plight was unknown to Father was also the recipient of this blessing. The little girl, Kirsty, also had asthma which seemed to improve right away. On her next visit to the doctor, there was no problem with the hips at all. And there hasn't been. At the time of this interview, this young lady was about twenty-two or twenty-three years old and she never had a problem with her hips again. A most interesting highlight however, is that Jim's dear daughter, Therese, who was six years old at the time, said something quite remarkable to Jim some time later; she said: "When Father blessed me, it felt like God was right there in the room." But it was not to her alone that this feeling came because Kirsty's mother also echoed: "And I felt the same thing."

Now, we must remember that Jim was a scientist and a man not given to exaggeration . He called things exactly as they were and added no embellishment. Thus, when he had a most unusual view of Father Aloysius during one of his visits, it surely seems that even though the scene was unique it must have been real-------While Jim and Father were talking, there came a lull in the conversation and as Jim looked at Father, he suddenly became: "Kind of fuzzy or diffused, and in his place-- and I saw it with these two eyes open--I saw him dressed as a Bishop with the purple robe and his face changed." Immediately after, Father again appeared back to normal and Jim said to him: "Father, I just saw you as a Bishop." To which Father replied: "Nonsense," or something like that. "He brushed that off in a hurry." Jim said.

Although he had heard about levitation, Jim had no personal experience of this with Father. But he did relate an interesting occurrence at the Claretian Center at 2208 West Eleventh Street in Los Angeles where Jim was working at this time under Father Richard Treviño as the Office Manager. Jim says: "One day, Father Richard came in and I heard the door open behind me and close behind me. I turned around and here's Father Richard Treviño, nobody else. I'm talking to a young lady, one of the workers here, and when I finished with her, I happened to turn around and there's Father Aloysius--and I didn't hear the door open and close again. So, we all got his blessing, Father Richard included, and I said: 'You want me to take you back up to the Provincial House, Father?' 'Yes.' So I took him back up to the Provincial House. How he got there, I don't know. Maybe he was back, clear back behind me some place and I didn't see him. But I doubt it because I looked around when Father Treviño came in."

As we were concluding the interview, Jim recalled one final event: "In 1959, Don Saben who lived three or four houses down the street had gangrene in one of his feet. While he was visiting with Jim, Father blessed him and the gangrene disappeared immediately. As Father was walking out of the house, he laid his hand on Jim's arm, stopped him for a moment and said: "You see Jim, how easy it is for God to do those things. He just struck that foot and it was well." Jim, too felt a reaction like a zap going through his body at the time of Father's blessing.

Surely there must be many more personal experiences and graces which Jim could have spoken of but how many more are necessary to show the intimate relationship which Jim, Mary and their family had with Father Aloysius. The names of three boys reflected that so well. There was John Aloysius, then Anthony, named for St. Anthony Mary Claret, and then the youngest was James Michael with Aloysius as his Confirmation name.

Mary died on March 8, 1987 from a recurring heart condition and Jim 's death from COPD was sixteen years later on September 17, 2003. They were both spared from the tragedy that took their oldest son, John who perished at the age of forty-three from the conflagration when the house caught fire on Oct 27, 2003.

Chapter Twenty-Two

<u>Marie Olk</u>

A trip to Calabasas, California on June 17, 1997 presented the opportunity to converse with Marie Olk. Although the interview was brief and spoke of no miraculous physical healing, it provided a remarkable insight into the working of the Holy Spirit.

Patricia Treece invited us to her home to meet her friend Marie Olk. Patricia who is a prominent Catholic author, knew that Marie would have an interesting story to tell. They had been friends for some time and now Patricia was sharing this friendship with us.

When Marie was quite young, her mother often related her stories about Father Aloysius whose Masses she had frequently attended. For years her mother told her about Father and spoke about him being a saintly man but Marie never really heard her. Although Marie practiced her faith, she did not accompany her mother to Father's Masses.

When Vatican II came along and many erroneous practices and interpretations ensued, Marie fell prey to these errors and left her Church. For approximately five years she remained involved in the New Age Movement which was in full swing at this time. It seemed that Marie's disillusionment with the Catholic Church was going to be adequately replaced with this new popular movement whose liberal and non dogmatic beliefs had made their appeal. This Movement embodies various fundamental beliefs which their followers may use as a shopping list for their own selection; thus they have a choice of beliefs and practices which provide individuals with the most personal comfort suitable for themselves. And these concepts are broad indeed in that they cover such aspects as Monism (a single source of divine energy produces all things), Pantheism (the entire universe is God), Reincarnation (there is repeated re-birth after death), Karma (we are reincarnated in a new life with reward or punishment according to the summation of our deeds), Universal Religion (there is no one correct religion), and New World Order (a new world government with no hunger, disease, or poverty, etc.), to name a few.

One day, Paula Kelly a friend of Marie, came to her with a request. Since it was rather obvious that Marie was going astray, Paula said: "Marie, I want you to go with me to see this Father Aloysius." Of course, the name immediately came back to Marie because she remembered how her mother had talked about him and thus she agreed to go with Paula.

Even though the name and location of the Church were not now to be recalled, it was surely the same place that Marie's mother had gone in years gone by. Marie described it as a small chapel with a lot of young people: "All kinds of people" were present. And they were all going to confession. Marie's words were: "There was just an incredible feeling of peace in that place----he touched me so deeply----I walked in----I had a conversion right there---it was incredible. It's been so many years and I still think about it." The anger and hostility of her previous environment was now replaced with tranquility and love. The conversion was completed when Father Alolysius heard Marie's confession. It was at that moment that she left the place where she had been for so long. She verified this when she said: "The Holy Spirit was in that place; you could just cut it with a knife. It was so peaceful there." She went on further to say: "He said the Mass with such reverence; I've never seen a Mass like that before---such reverence." Then in his homily, Marie quotes Father as saying: "I don't want you people elevating me. You know it hurts me when you do that. Don't do that to me. If you continue to do that, I'm going to be sent away." Marie said: "He was so humble; he didn't want people making him a saint or anything special. He just felt he was a priest." After this turning point in her life, Marie began attending daily Mass and got more and more involved in the Church. The Holy Spirit had used this humble, holy instrument of His as the means of conferring the grace necessary to pull a soul out of modern day confusion.

Chapter Twenty-Three

Reyes and Estela Ruiz

On January 25, 1991 as one of several interviews in Phoenix, Arizona, we began an extensive dialogue and inquiry into the lives of Reyes and Estela Ruiz. Although their name was the same, they were no relatives of Father Alberto Ruiz.

Local and national prominence had been given to this couple because of their unusual devotion and leadership in Catholic community activity. Their simple but comfortable home was to be our domain for many hours.

Reyes was the spokesman and gave a lengthy introduction wherein he recounted his early days, providing emphasis on his calling to the spiritual life and his response to this calling. He was a firm advocate of Marian devotion through the years. Even though he thought this devotion to have peaked within himself, he seemed to enter a magnificent new phase when he was privileged to hear of and subsequently meet Father Aloysius when Father came to Phoenix.

Actually, Reyes developed his love for the Blessed Virgin Mary when he was despondent, having just lost his father in an automobile accident. Mystified by the Lord's apparent cruelty in having taken his father, Reyes searched for solace and found it in Mary. He was mad with God and felt that he had to turn to somebody and Mary was the person to whom he had seen priests turn.

Aloysius

She was a beautiful woman who would listen to him. Although he loved Our Lord, he couldn't find in Him this real love for which he was searching. Yet his devotion to Mary was over abundant.

When Reyes met Father Aloysius, he had just finished a Cursillo where he was enamored with Mary but still searching for Jesus. In Father Aloysius, Reyes felt the presence of somebody special. He knew there was something about him but he couldn't describe it. Their common devotion to Mary was the bond which impelled Reyes. Father Aloysius acceded to his wishes and became his spiritual director for the next three years. They would meet twice a week and their relationship was a relationship of prayer. Reyes was astounded because he discovered that prayer was the most beautiful means of communication between people and their God. In his three years with Father Aloysius, Reyes found out that Father had something that he himself did not have: Father Aloysius had Our Lord. Reyes now realized that Father had something to give him. He observed Father in prayer in a manner so deep that he really wasn't there anymore. Here was the embodiment of a relationship with God that Reyes was seeking. In all these years of coming to him: "he taught me the meaning of prayer. He taught me the enjoyment of the Rosary." The impact of this teaching was so immediate that it caused Reyes to enter St. Catherine Church and spend two hours before the Blessed Sacrament saying the Rosary. Such an event was so elating to Reyes that he raced to share his exuberance with Father who then countered with his beautiful smile.

In his own inimical way, Reyes explained how Father Aloysius imbued in him a heightened spirituality. This was not by preaching, because Reyes described Father as being a "terrible preacher." But what a beautiful message did he deliver in his saying of the Holy Mass! Father Aloysius would be completely lost in the Mass---it was as though it could go on forever. Repeatedly, Reyes was at a loss for words in his effort to describe his joy with the relationship that he had been seeking and had now found with the Lord. Many people had spoken of Father Aloysius being "elevated" when he was celebrating the Eucharist. Reyes could not verify this as being a true occurrence because he was too engrossed in the Sacrament itself that he was too busy to ever take notice. Whether he would "elevate" or not "It didn't make any difference because I was enjoying the Eucharist;" as Reyes described his exhilaration. Now indeed, Father Aloysius had become the instrument of his spiritual growth. Overcome by emotion, Reyes could hardly speak of his inner feelings.

After Father Aloysius left Phoenix, Reyes never saw him again. Only once did he phone Father but spiritually he remained in contact seeking his blessings on all of his endeavors. When Reyes' grandfather suffered from cancer, Reyes gave him a rosary which Father Aloysius had previously given to him. For twenty-two years this rosary remained with the grandfather. After his death, it returned to Reyes, somewhat disheveled but still a prized possession. When Reyes went to Medjugorje in September of 1988, he took this rosary along with about forty others. Of this group, only one rosary turned golden---it was the particular rosary that had been given to Reyes by Father.

Reyes displayed a picture of Our Lady which Father Aloysius had given to him twenty-seven years ago. This was somewhat of a mystery to him; he did not understand what the picture meant or what it was supposed to do. Its significance was a mystery. On one occasion, a doctor who was visiting at the house, gazed at the picture and gave a comment which others too had given--- at times, the countenance of Our Lady changes into the likeness of Our Lord and then back again as before. Routinely, Reyes placed this picture in room after room with no apparent approval of Estela.

Reyes felt that on occasion the Blessed Mother must have appeared to Father Aloysius and what's more that he had knowledge of upcoming events. He believed in retrospect that he was being prepared for those upcoming events that were going to take place in his house. Reyes became an ardent worker in his diocese and gave away many rosaries. One day when he sought to give a rosary to a visiting man, he could find none. Never one to quit, he asked for help and before the day was over, he had been given one thousand rosaries. In total, he thinks that he has given out seventeen thousand rosaries and delights in the fact that if the recipients of these rosaries complied with Reyes request for prayers, he would have received seventeen thousand Hail Marys. He felt in constant contact with Father Aloysius and Our Blessed Lady. Even at the infrequent parish dances that he attended, he found himself looking at the people and trying to imagine who among them would Our Lady resemble if she were here.

Just as Father Aloysius experienced the presence of the Lord himself, so also did he teach Reyes to seek this companionship. The instruction to Reyes was in the form of Spiritual Communion. Never are we to be without the presence of Jesus in our daily activities. We must learn to make a Spiritual Communion and then do so many times during the day. This practice sunk in very deeply with Reyes so that his days were full of Spiritual Communions. For Reyes, this teaching was the most significant one that he was given through his many meetings with Father.

Reyes stated that he could feel the presence of the Holy Eucharist within Father and therefore he understood why he had become so enamored with this Jesus---the God that he had never really known for so many years---the God who through Father had taught him that prayer was so necessary for the salvation of souls. Now there was real joy, ecstatic joy, within his heart because of his new dear friend.

When Reyes completed his story, my wife Mary asked Estela to tell how she and Reyes had first met. It seems that this occurred when Estela was 15 and Reyes was 18. They became good friends for five years before they were married. With a very strict mother, Estela was the only girl in her family with three older brothers.

Estela and Reyes' first child, a son, was followed by a set of twins, then a daughter, and a son and the final child, a daughter. Estela and Reyes worked in the Cursillo movement for several years until Estela realized that she needed to devote full time to her growing family. She therefore began assisting at St. Catherine School. During the time that Father Aloysius was spiritual director for Reyes, Estela met Father and attended some of his Masses but she didn't get to know him very well. On some of Reyes' visits to Father, the children came along and thus they also were able to meet him and reveled in his friendship. Estela had heard about Father through some friends and didn't seem too interested in pursuing a relationship because her upbringing had taught her to shy away from supernatural events which may possibly be superstitious. Estela received blessings from Father but did not participate in his counseling. She felt that Reyes was doing what was best for him and that she should devote her time to the children. That was her whole life; she lived for her children.

As the children grew older and advanced in school, Estela felt she had to do something different. She seemed to get caught up in the women's liberation atmosphere and talked to Reyes about going to work. She immediately got a job in the school system and from there, things began to move in her favor. Having been given the directorship of a small bi-lingual program, her activities increased and she even started back to school herself to fulfill a dream she had been seeking. In time, she received her teaching degree. Meanwhile, her children had married and had now provided her and Reyes with grandchildren. She soon found her niche as a director in the school system. She was motivated by increased pay and fascination with her job. Her attention now moved away from her home, her husband and her children; she was caught up in a career. She wanted to embark on higher education and advance up the ladder.

Soon they adopted a little boy Tony, and decided to move to a different house in hopes of setting up a business. They made this decision in 1986. Then, one year later, Reyes read an article about Our Blessed Mother appearing in Yugoslavia. He was interested in the article and shared it with Estela but it didn't appeal to her. At that time, Estela began putting "our God to one side because it wasn't the thing to do when you're in business. God doesn't come into the picture." She says that she thinks her God had become her work. Her days were fully occupied with her job. The more time she gave, the more money she got and the more prestige she was given. Within, she knew: "They can't do without me, I run that program; you know how important I am at that work."

When Reyes asked if she would like to accompany him to Medjugorje, Estela expressed disinterest. She even thought that Reyes was a very strange man. The more spiritual he became, the more strange did he appear. She actually stated that: "This is a weird man. He prays all day, he has that rosary in his hand continuously, I think he overdoes it." She told her children: "Your dad is a very, very weird man. He seems to talk to Our Blessed Mother." After they had been to a dance, he told Estela the next day that he was thinking that he would have liked to have been dancing with Our Blessed Mother. She thought this was sacrilegious and said: "Lord have mercy, this man is crazy, he must have a strange idea of what religion is ......this is not word of God. I never believed in the supernatural; I didn't like to think about it. I was fearfully afraid of the devil. I didn't even like to say his name. If I don't think of him he is not engaged in my life. With that intent, I put him out of my life..... I was kind of like in between. I didn't want to know about the devil but then I also wanted to be involved with God. I was walking the fence. I didn't want to be too much involved; I went to Sunday Mass. I felt that should be enough, not that I ever stopped loving God. I began to give more attention to things that were not of God." As she looks back on it now, she feels that the Blessed Mother had a very devoted son but his wife needed a lot of work.

Reyes didn't give up on Medjugorje, he said: "Come on, let's go." Once again, Estela turned him down saying: "No, you go." So, he made the decision that he was going to make the trip without her. But he was quite repetitive in his suggestion that Estela give him a petition that he could give to the Blessed Mother for something that she would like. She replied: "I don't need anything, I have a wonderful job, they pay me plenty money, I'm doing the thing I like to do. I didn't think of my children at that time because my mind was not working at that level." However, they had a son who was addicted to drugs but she had given up on him after he had been in and out of rehab. She told him: "I don't want to see you again because if you want to take your life away, then that's your decision. Don't come back here until you give it up." There were a lot of things that she needed to pray for but she wasn't doing it because she was "caught up." Estela could think of no special petition for Reyes to take with him, but finally she did think of herself. She was very fearful of dying. She had a tremendous fear of death. It was troublesome for her to even think that one day she would die. She colored her hair so that she wouldn't remember that she "was getting closer to the other side." Every two weeks she worked at this hair project. She didn't want to be reminded of forthcoming death and she didn't want anybody else to think of it. Right before Reyes left, he said: "You've got to ask for something." So, she wrote on a piece of paper: "Take the fear of death away from me." While she was writing, the thought occurred to her that she might as well ask for the big thing, so she added: "And make sure that I go to heaven when I die." So, in September of 1988, Reyes left on his trip.

It wasn't long before Estela began to experience the response to her petition. She awoke one morning and felt that something was happening to her. She remembers going into the kitchen and she heard a voice saying: "Good morning, daughter." Surprised and confused, she talked herself out of it and continued on her day's journey and went to work. Then, three or four days later, with Reyes still at Medjugorje, she went by the picture of Our Lady Of Guadalupe and once again heard: "Good morning, my daughter." I turned and I said: "Good morning, Blessed Mother." "When I heard myself answer, it scared me, because I thought, my goodness, I'm getting weird and strange as my husband. I think I'm talking to the Blessed Mother." Estela was so surprised with herself that she thought: "I don't even want to think about this." "I just ignored it." She said. She returned to her routine, woke up Tony, their adopted son, went to work and forgot it.

Then Reyes returned home, and people began to come to the Ruiz house to hear about the apparitions at Medjugorje. When Reyes talked to the visiting people and spoke of the beautiful things that were happening there and told of the joy, Estela sat there and listened in total awe. Every time that people came to hear Reyes speak, she would sit there and listen. Soon, she was able to prompt Reyes in his delivery to remind him of the things that he had forgotten to mention. It was as though she had made the trip with him.

Then, Estela began to feel a "real moving back to God." This was an abrupt change for her. In the past, she thought that Reyes had been pushing her to embrace his spiritual life but she resisted then because she felt like she had her own devotion and it was sufficient. Now, with this sudden change, she woke up one morning in adequate time to accompany Reyes to morning Mass. Her previous refusals to go with him had now vanished. This sudden motivation seemed strange to her. When she informed Reyes that she was going with him, he looked at her in great surprise, wondering, as Estela puts it: "What in the world is going on here?" She got ready, went to Mass, came home, and went to work. No problem! The next morning, the same thing happened. Day after day, Estela would hear something tell her to go to Mass: "You need to go to Mass." And she in reply would say: "I need to go to Mass." Things began to really change in her life. Not only in her life did a change take place, but also in the lives of the children. They came over and spoke of the calling that they too had received from the Blessed Mother to a deeper spiritual life. Their son, Armando, who is thirty-three now, had a marriage problem and he also came over expressing a similar urge.

Estela says she fell in love with the Blessed Mother and recalled then her previous attitude wherein she had been jealous of Our Lady because Reyes gave her so much attention. She admonished Reyes at that time because she saw the love that he had been giving to her as love that was actually being denied to Our Blessed Lord, a common misbelief. Not so now, with her. She knew that she had been badly mistaken. It was useless for her now to fight this impulse of Our Lady.

One day Reyes requested Estela to sit and talk about their children and the need to guide them to a new spiritual life. "They're not going to listen to us." She replied. "They haven't listened to us; I don't know what we can do." Not totally captured yet by Our Lady, she still felt a bit attracted to her job. "I really don't know what we can do," she said, as she walked away from Reyes. As she turned around, she saw tears rolling down his cheeks. With remorse, she said to herself: "How can I be so cruel? I don't even know what he wants me to do. Why don't I tell him this? So, I came back and sat down and said: 'Reyes. I don't know what you want me to do, but whatever it is you want me to do, I will do it. I will help you. I don't even know what it is but I will do it.'" As he wiped his tears away, he thanked her profusely.

That night when Reyes awakened and said his Rosary, Estela saw him get back in bed and quickly go to sleep. She hoped that she too would go back to sleep again. She did sleep, and then dreamed that Our Blessed Mother was going to appear to her and Reyes. She saw a bright light come into her room. She shook Reyes telling him that the Blessed Mother was going to appear to them. With a mild reaction, he calmed her anxiety and assured her that it was all right for her to appear. Then, Estela went in and out of sleep. In that milieu, she soon saw Reyes and the Blessed Mother conversing while she slept. The image that Estela saw was identical to the holy card which she now held in her hand. It showed the classic picture of the Immaculate Conception as seen by St. Catherine Labouré except that the rays were now missing. "I went crazy, I began to cry;" she said. All of this happened in her dream. She was ecstatic, proclaiming: "How beautiful you are Blessed Mother. You are so beautiful, I love you, I love you." Then Estela continued: "At that moment she turned to me, she looked at me, I saw her beautiful face and then in an instant it changed, it was the face of my mother who died in 1977. It was her face. Then, I thought, my mother! Then it changed back, it was her beautiful face. Then I began to reach out to her to try to touch her. She began to reach out to me but I never could touch her. Then I woke up and looked around, what a beautiful dream! I felt my heart full, full of joy. Something wonderful has happened to me. Then I put my head back on the pillow and fell asleep." The next morning she told Reyes: "I think the Blessed Mother appeared to us. "When she discussed the dream with Reyes she really didn't know if any part of the dream was real. Reyes explained simply that the Blessed Mother could do anything that she wanted to do.

Estela went to work and felt like she was floating; she followed her normal routine and handled matters properly yet she felt like she wasn't really there. She wanted to be thinking of the Blessed Mother constantly. She believed that she now had the love for Our Lady just as Father Aloysius had it. She then told her son, Armando that she was going to go to the Religious Store and get the most beautiful Rosary that she could find. At the store she bought what she was looking for, a beautiful silver Rosary. But there too, she excitedly called

Armando's attention to a picture of Our Lady that she had spotted. It was just like the view that she had in the dream. On the other side of the picture she saw a novena. Her immediate response to this leaflet was her resolution to say a novena. Her devotion was increasing and she resolved to pray the daily Rosary as well. Previously, the family had been saying the Rosary on Sundays, but now the frequency had changed. Without forcing the children to do so, the family Rosary was recited daily in Reyes' and Estela's home. Another event was also in action: Reyes began painting a picture of Our Lady. In about a week he had it completed. The picture now was prominently displayed on the wall as we spoke. It showed the facial features of Our Lady just as Estela had seen them in her dream. She was amazed that Reyes had pictured Our Lady in that manner even though he had not seen her.

In October, several days after experiencing the joy of the picture, Reyes now informed Estela that he felt like he had to give the picture away. This broke her heart. She said that she was not a crying woman but now she found herself crying on the slightest provocation. To her, Reyes cried about everything, now she had become like him.

During the rest of the month of November they continued with their prayers and Estela had now grown to know within herself the same love for Our Lady that had previously been so foreign. "She stole my heart completely;" she said.

On December 3, 1988, the last day of their novena to the Blessed Mother, as they prayed the Rosary in Estela's bedroom, she felt the Blessed Mother calling for her. "Oh no", she felt, "I'm going to have the same thing happen to me that happened with Our Lady of Guadalupe." She tried to ignore it. But that night she began to pray for her children. She began to pray more and to talk to Our Lady and told her that her children were not living right and that she could not control them. With confidence, she told Our Lady that she herself could do that. "I can't stop them because they're too old. If I give them to you, you can. I give them to you this night. They have been consecrated to you since they were babies. They are your children. I give them completely to you." In order not to be distracted from her prayer, Estela closed her eyes and continued to talk to Our Lady. As she would close and then open her eyes again, she was always drawn to the picture on the wall. She experienced a strange feeling and her heart began to pound within her.

At the conclusion of the Rosary, a daughter-in-law began to start it over in Spanish. This prompted Estela to give her entreaty in behalf of her children to Our Lady once again. This time she did it in Spanish. Then when she opened her eyes again and gazed at the picture, she was suddenly unable to close them, as though they were paralyzed. She now saw a tremendous bright light shining all around the picture. Estela couldn't move. She wanted to speak to those around her but she was unable to do so. At that moment, Our Blessed Mother stepped right out of the picture and stood before her, smiling. No matter how hard she tried, she could not speak and announce the vision to her family. All she could do was clutch her Rosary. Then Our Lady spoke and said: "Don't you know that I am going to take care (of your children)?" Estela then began to cry exactly as she had done in her dream. Even throughout Estela's excitement,

Reyes continued praying the Rosary. Although he could not see the vision, he and the children knew something was going on. They could feel her presence in the room. They estimated it took about three minutes. Estela remembers Our Blessed Mother saying: "I'm going to leave now." And she didn't know what the future held for her. She then read the contents of her novena leaflet to us and told of her concerns. She thought that the Blessed Mother would be coming back but she feared that she would then ask Estela for something and she dreaded this thought.

Estela then discussed her cares with a priest who told her that he too thought Our Lady would return and ask her something. His advice was that she could always say no, if she wanted to do so and The Blessed Mother would not love her any less for that. "Father, how in the world, after seeing the most beautiful woman, could I possibly say no, to her; to see those beautiful eyes, how could I possibly say, no," was her reply to the priest. He said: "Well, that's a decision you're going to have to make." So, Estela resolved that she would give a favorable reply if she were requested to do something.

On December 7, 1988, "Our Lady appeared again and she asked me if I would be her messenger, because she wanted to use me in that way." She would give me the strength. She said that I would be able to do it if I would say yes. She will always be with me and she would guide me. I would be her spokesperson. I said: "How would they believe me. They won't believe me."----"Yes they will. Yes, they will believe you." And sure enough, they did.

The Blessed Mother let Estela know that her family was in her domain. Her oldest son had been "kind of working in another church." But Our Lady assured Estela that he was going to be all right. I have learned a lot of things from Our Blessed Mother. And one of the things that she has learned is what a special man Father Aloysius is. Estela said: "She told me that he was a saint; that he is a saint." The reason that the Blessed Mother made this statement was because of Estela's inquiry. Whenever the Blessed Mother appeared to Estela, she could feel the presence of Father Aloysius and speak to him asking for his intercession to obtain strength. Estela had not known Father very well; he became her friend after death.

It was quite obvious that more and more Our Lady became a vibrant force in Estela's life. She expressed it herself, saying: "She's brought great joy into my life. She's also brought great suffering; that's OK."

The first few times she would cry to the Blessed Mother and say: Why me, Blessed Mother, why not my husband? He had the devotion. Not me." Then Estela mentioned that she has a very good sense of humor; one time she told me: "Would you have believed him if he had told you?" I said: "No." She said: "That's one reason. There's other reasons, that's not the only reason. There has to be a visible conversion that would be believable. I don't want you to ask me anymore because when I come and get you after death, you will know why. You were chosen a long time ago, so don't worry about that " Therefore, she didn't worry about it anymore.

The Blessed Mother told Estela that she doesn't want to have an image of her without the image of her son also there. "My son always has to be there because He is the way to salvation." Estela emphasized the fact that one cannot love the Blessed Mother without loving her Son and also you cannot love Him without loving her. That is the love that Reyes was talking about. We must consecrate ourselves to the Sacred Heart of her Son.

When my wife Mary, asked Estela about her job, she said that the end of her contract year was in June of 1989. By that time people had been coming to pray with them. The reporters came from the newspaper and they were also on television but only after the reporter agreed with Estela's terms. Before there could be any interview, he had to come over to her house and pray with them. So that is what he did. He came over on that Saturday night and stayed until two in the morning. When they were praying, Estela asked the Blessed Mother to give him one of her beautiful smiles. Then later when she spoke to the reporter, they discussed the picture that was so prominently displayed for them to see. Estela said that she didn't know if the Blessed Mother had given the smile that she had requested but at that point, the reporter spoke of the beautiful smile which he noticed on the Blessed Mother's face in the picture. But Estela knew that there is no smile there and strived to emphasize that point. He would not agree. Even after he had gone out of the door to go home, he came back in and insisted that the Blessed Mother had smiled at him in the portrait. At 2:00 A.M. he was still convinced of what he had seen earlier.

The reporter wrote a beautiful article about the Ruiz family in the newspaper and then did another beautiful report when the miracle of the sun appeared at Estela's house. In fact, that miracle was captured on video tape and broadcast over the air.

When a commission was set up to investigate the apparitions, it was recommended that Reyes and Estela get a spiritual director. So they sought out Father Frank Ambrosi whom Reyes had known for several years in El Paso. But at that time, Father Ambrosi was being transferred to Fresno.

Nevertheless, they prayed to the Blessed Mother to get Father Ambrosi. They needed a very spiritual man and Father Ambrosi was just that. They contacted Father Alberto and asked if they could contact Father Ambrosi in Fresno. Then he let them in on a little secret. Father Ambrosi was going to be transferred to Phoenix. Therefore, in response to Estela and Reyes' prayers, Father Ambrosi had now been located just five minutes away. "Thank you, my Mother, you are bringing him here," Estela told Our Lady.

It was not uncommon for both Father Ambrosi and Father Mario to be visitors to the Ruiz home.

Exactly two hours after our interview had begun, we concluded our first segment.

Reyes says that when Our Lady appeared the second time, he asked Estela to ask her who she was and who sent her. On December 10, while the bishop was celebrating the Mass, Estela did this at Immaculate Heart of Mary Church, (where Father Aloysius had been for three years when he came to Phoenix) and Our Lady told her: "Look around, look around." When Estela looked around, she could see the pictures of all the apparitions that Our Lady had had----the way she had appeared in different countries. When Estela looked at them, she told her: "I am all of them, but I have come as the Immaculate Heart of Mary."

Estela then told Reyes concerning Our Lady's picture which he had painted: "Put a heart on it." But Reyes said: "You'd better ask her because I know that woman and I know what she would like and you better ask her what she wants. So Estela asked her and she said "No, all of you are my heart." When Our Lady told them that all of the people were her heart, Reyes decided to make a large heart composed of many, many photos of the individual people within.

In the summertime in the evening, the yard was packed with visitors. In order to accommodate the huge crowd and give an appropriate setting for the devotions that were taking place at the Ruiz residence, Reyes began constructing a shrine.

On Tuesday, June 17, 1989 Our Lady appeared and said that she wanted the shrine that Reyes was building to be done by Saturday. Reyes's response to Estela when he received that news was:"Obviously, she has never been in construction." One of Reyes' sons offered the commentary: "Her Son was in construction, he was a carpenter."

Reyes finished all of the concrete work on time and at a later date put more elaborate finishing on the altar.

Aloysius

To answer our inquiry about the devotions that were
attended in the yard by the masses of people who came
from everywhere, Reyes said that when the people gather
in the yard, there will be two readings from Scripture,
first in English and then in Spanish. This will be
followed by the Rosary being recited by five different
people to allow their participation.

The Ruiz family had acquired several adjacent properties
to provide room for the hundreds of people who
participated in the devotions. Reyes credits Our Lady as
being into real estate since he himself was unable to buy
one of the properties without her help.

Reyes said that during the day whenever Estela goes into
prayer, Our Lady appears to her and dictates a message
to her for the people. Then they put it into the computer,
and print it into both languages for Estela to give to the
people after the Rosary.

However, during the Rosary, Our Lady appears again to
Estela and sometime her message is for some individual.
Indeed, during the afternoon, such was the case during
our visit. Estela handed me a message which The Blessed
Mother had dictated to her for Mary and me:

MESSAGE FROM OUR LADY OF THE AMERICAS
JANUARY 26, 1991

My Dear Little Ones, Francis and Mary,
        I thank you so much on this day for your love of
God and for your love of my son Aloysius. He was, and
continues to be, a true son of My Immaculate Heart, and

158

a true son of God. I had much love for him because he was an obedient son of God. The Lord lived in his heart, and he lived in the love of God. He brought many souls to My Son, Jesus, especially in the Eucharist, and was therefore very favored in Our Father's eyes.

I thank you greatly for your commitment in letting many know of his love of God because in honoring Him you honor God. You do so because my favored son, Aloysius, was a true servant of God and was, and will continue to be, a model for my children here on earth.

Know that I am with you at every moment of your work. I bless you for your commitment and give you my love in gratitude. Continue the work you are doing and know that you have Our Lord's blessings as you carry on your work.

As one of his final messages to us, Reyes said they are very careful in trying to discern what is happening when events occur that very well could be the working of the devil.

Before we departed, we had the privilege of sharing a roundtable discussion with Reyes, Estela, Fr. Ambrosi and Doctor and Mrs. Junck.

Many years later, on September 1, 2011, the writer contacted Estela in Phoenix and learned that her husband Reyes had died in 2003 and now she is devoted to Catholic ministry in Phoenix and other cities throughout the world.

Chapter Twenty-Four

A Particular Story

The impetus for the many recorded interviews contained herein was the personal experiences which the writer had had. So overwhelming and spiritually uplifting was this personal association with Father Aloysius that it inspired the activity of subsequent years to portray the sanctity and humanness of this priest as a beacon to all. At this time, in order to best illustrate the individual story which this writer has to relate, a previously written book has to be referenced. Essentially, this story, first told in 1986, has been self published in book form entitled "Our Guide," but to add notoriety, this book is synthesized herein. In its original form, Father Charles Carpenter, M.A.P. generously provided a Foreword and Bishop Juan Arzube of Los Angeles, a close friend of Father Aloysius, gave his own recommendation for this text. Following then, is the story which the writer tells as an addition to the numerous interviews which he conducted.

Our Guide

Throughout my life I have been singularly blessed by having holy priests in close association. It was the Oblates of Mary Immaculate who served in my home parish in New Orleans and administered the primary school that I attended. Hard working Irish and American priests were exemplary workers in the vineyard. During high school and college, I was trained by the Jesuits and had some excellent cleric and lay educators. In later years, I relied particularly on the Fathers of the Sacred Hearts. It was while in their midst that I was confronted with the tragic and spiritually awakening era of my life. Most recently, however, I became attached to the Claretians.

It is obvious to me now, that the Lord knew from the very beginning that I would need the best of help in order to guide me; so He never hesitated to provide. In times of greatest need, I could always be sure that God would hear my prayers. A vivid example was in 1950, in Bremerton, Washington during the Korean War (which had been the reason for my recall to naval service). I was assigned to a ship which was still in "moth balls" and was being re-activated for service. It was hardly habitable; therefore, portions of the crew including myself were permitted to live ashore. Realizing that I might never come back from this war alive, I seized the opportunity to have my wife, Marion, travel from New Orleans with me on this assignment to share a few weeks together. Our only child was left at home in the care of our parents, and Marion was in the latter stages of pregnancy with our second child. The weather was dismal, rainy and depressing; our quarters were in a simple motel along the road outside of town. In our last few days before I was sent with this ship overseas, while it was still being renovated, I left Marion at the motel one Sunday morning and obtained a ride with someone to the navy base for a day of duty aboard ship as Officer of the Deck. I told Marion that if she wanted to go to church, she would have to hitchhike for we had no car. That she did, willingly, even with her physical discomfort. As a means of remaining together spiritually, we had swapped Rosaries -- my wooden beads had become hers and her large crystal beads with the ornate silver crucifix had become mine. Having boarded the ship to begin my duty, I dismissed the two enlisted men who were on watch at the gangway. I figured it was a good time for them to go below decks to the galley for coffee. Soon thereafter, I entered the officer's restroom and closed the door. Immediately, I noticed that the knob and shaft were missing, and the door was hopelessly locked. Realizing that no one else was on this entire deck, I knew that shouting or noise making would be fruitless; prayer alone would free me. Thus, I spoke briefly but confidently in prayer to Our Lady: "Dear Blessed Mother, if you want me to remain locked in this room, I will accept your will and wait until tomorrow when many people come aboard, and then surely, I will be found; or, Blessed Mother, if you see fit, please let me out, so that I may go about my duties." I said one Hail Mary. Then, I looked around this compartment and noticed only barren bulkheads, devoid of any implements. Nowhere could I find a device which could be used to pry the door open. So I decided to look into my pockets to see what type of tool I might have with me. When I reached into my first pocket there surely was no tool there. Here I found Marion's Rosary. Perplexed, but undaunted, I held the Rosary in my hand and examined it briefly. It presented one tool for my use: the ornate crucifix which it had was the exact size to fit diagonally into the door latch. When I positioned it there and turned it as though it were a tool, the door opened easily. Ardently thankful to Our Lady for her prompt assistance , I was now free to go about my duties aboard ship.

Why, then, if Our Blessed Lady heard me so readily on this and other occasions, would she not hasten to help me later in life when I was in dire need. Surely, as a truly solicitous Mother she would send Father Aloysius, a most holy son of hers, to guide me. Yes, he would be my spiritual advisor for twenty years and share with me the sad and the joyful moments that were to transpire. Countless others too would experience the effects of an encounter with this mystic priest. He would see Victor and Irma Dueñas, Marion's parents, celebrate their 50th wedding anniversary with his blessing. Albert and Henrietta Levy, my parents, were also to be the fortunate recipients of Father's blessing. Father Aloysius Ellacuria, C.M.F., a pious and humble Spanish missionary, a holy man of God, became my "Spiritual Father," and he filled me with joy when he called me his "Spiritual Son." How these events were to take place will be seen as the story unfolds.

TRAGEDY

During November of 1960, it was on the tenth of the month, as I recall, my wife, Marion, had a biopsy performed at Pomona Valley Hospital in Pomona, California. Our sixth child, Ann, had been born a year earlier, exactly ten years after her oldest brother, Frank, thus completing a three time repeat of the boy - girl cycle. And it was in Ann that we had a brunette to go along with blonde Linda and the red haired Gail. We had a beautiful family for which I was thankful, but what was going to happen to it now? I knew well the ominous threat of a biopsy for Marion herself was a nurse. California had been our new home for only five years. At last, after years of struggling economically in New Orleans, the opportunity had come for professional advancement and the easing of financial pressure. Thus, we didn't delay when I was offered a job in this prosperous locale. This sudden turn of events was traumatic.

After hours of surgery, I was confronted by Drs. Naujokaitis and Crowley who came to announce their terrible findings. I was alone in the hospital as they spoke to me, and it was dreadfully alone and abandoned that I felt.

Yes, the lump in the breast was malignant, and a simple mastectomy had been performed. The prognosis was not good, only time would tell.   I was tempted to anger and I didn't hesitate to let the Lord know how wrong He had been. Yet I prayed to Him just in case He wanted to change His mind. I went to our pastor, Father James Keefe, SS.CC., and begged for his prayers. My parents, brothers and sisters, always devoted and prayerful, never neglected me or mine in their heavenly solicitations. The Daughters of Charity of Saint Vincent de Paul (three of my sisters are in this order) and the Oblates of Mary Immaculate, who have a priest brother of mine, prayed for us as did many other religious and lay groups.

Immediate chemotherapy produced a violent reaction. Then, neither radiation therapy nor the subsequent oophorectomy were able to stem the spread of cancer, but during this period we were blessed by a continuous series of events.

Priorities suddenly had changed. No longer were those demands of yesterday even to be remembered. I was now seized by apprehension and fear.

THE PAINFUL JOURNEY

During her convalescence from her initial surgery in November 1960, while I was at work one day, Marion was visited by a priest from Spain whose name I do not know. He was brought to our house by a woman, whose name also I do not know. She lived in Our Lady of Talpa parish in Los Angeles, where Maxine my eldest sister, a nun, had been stationed a few years earlier. This priest was anxious to spread devotion to Saint Anthony Mary Claret, the founder of the Claretian Order, a Religious group that I had never before heard of. The prayer which he left with Marion was a common leaflet, apparently printed in Spain. The net result of this visit was that Marion added this leaflet to her group of daily prayers, and we both disregarded the incident as nothing more than pious solicitude on the part of our visitors. Several weeks later, however, the woman wrote to Marion saying that she would be glad to introduce her to Father Aloysius. Since we had never heard of this priest (the superior at the Claretian Provincial House in Los Angeles), and since we had our own parish priests nearby, I tended to politely dismiss this opportunity. Coincidentally, Mary Greene's daughter, Maureen, had recently stopped by with a holy article from Fr. Aloysius, and also, on the very same day that the letter came, Marion received a call from Mary Greene, who recommended that we attend Fr. Aloysius' novena on Sundays in Los Angeles. Mrs. Greene also stated that if we needed a ride, Dr. Herbert Morrow's wife, Katherine, would be glad to take us.

At this point, it seemed that everybody was impressed by Father Aloysius except me. Out of curiosity, I took Marion to the novena in the old structure that was the Claretian

Provincial House at 1119 Westchester Place. The novena was to be held in a very small chapel off of the main parlor at about 2 o'clock. The place was packed; the crowd overflowed from the chapel to the area outside of the doorway, a library, and over into the parlor. It was in this parlor that Marion and I were standing when Father Aloysius came down the steps and into the crowd. On numerous occasions in future years, he was to recount this first visual contact with me, even though I was unknown to him and surely he was unknown to me.

Father proceeded with the novena to the Blessed Mother and prayed to Saint Anthony Claret. After the service, he blessed each of the people there individually by placing his hands on their head. When he came to Marion, she spoke quietly to him, telling him that she had cancer, and he said that he would like us to come see him during the week. I was working fifty miles away in Pomona at the time, and I thought it would be difficult to get time off to visit Father, but it turned out to be surprisingly easy. However, we never would have gone without an invitation. In fact, this first private visit was the beginning of many weekday visits (about on the average of twice a week), each visit being with his earnest invitation.

During our first visit, Father took Marion and me into the chapel where we prayed. Father was using his Rosary, and I was greatly impressed by his devotion as he clutched his beads. In fact, I was so impressed that I silently hoped to have his Rosary for my very own. Shortly after we left the chapel, Father spoke to us and said as he turned to Marion: "I want you to have the Rosary that I used." With that, he presented his Rosary to her. In amazement I turned to Father and said: "My prayer was answered even better than

I had hoped; I wanted the Rosary for myself, but you gave it to my wife."

The Rosary which Father had given to Marion was a specially indulgenced one which had been given to him. He had very few of them, but he left the room for several moments and soon returned with one for me as well. Father was very interested in these particular Rosaries since they had a special Indulgence applicable to the souls in Purgatory. Because of his interest in these Rosaries, I left not a stone unturned investigating a means of supplying them for him. Thus did he receive many. Marion cherished her special Rosary, and at her death I saw to it that she was buried with it.

On each visit, Father's blessings were long and intense. Most of the time, I experienced an overwhelming spiritual sensation during his blessing. It was as though the Lord Himself were present. Almost always, a distinct fragrant aroma surrounded Father. On one occasion I went into the chapel to pray and noticed that Father Aloysius was also kneeling in prayer. He concluded his prayers, and I was left alone in the chapel. In a few moments I was distracted by the characteristic aroma, which I immediately attributed to flowers apparently in the garden outside. By looking completely around the chapel, however, I learned that there were no windows open, and there were no flowers inside either. Why, then, the aroma? Soon, it dawned on me that even though Father had left, his aroma lingered for several minutes. It was this fragrance that I had erroneously attributed to flowers.

Although we prayed hard, and Father blessed us frequently at his Sunday novenas and during our numerous weekday visits, Marion's condition grew steadily worse. In total desperation, I prayed at home privately one night: "Lord, what would You have me do?" A few days later, when we were visiting Father, he was explaining to us the splendor of the Angels and what their mission is. Marion and I were seated, and Father's eyes were directed at her. Suddenly, in the midst of his explanation, he turned to me and said: "God would have you do no more than you are doing." Dumbfounded, I addressed Father and said: "Do you realize that you have answered my prayer exactly as I said it? Father smiled and cast his eyes downward, as he would usually do in humility.

THE ANGELS

Father was very devoted to the Angels and taught us to say the Angelic Chaplet. Through the years, we learned that: The Angels are composed of nine Choirs: the Seraphim (whom Father often described as being a pure flame), Cherubim, Thrones, Dominations, Virtues, Powers, Principalities, Archangels, and Angels. The duties of these Choirs are: The Seraphim are given to the love of God; they are pure love and occupy the highest position among the Choirs. The Cherubim exemplify knowledge, and they stand next in rank below the Seraphim, Father also mentioned that some people have Seraphim and even St. Michael, too, as Guardian Angels. It seems that he meant these special Angels as additional to the regularly assigned Guardian Angels. The third Choir, the Thrones, are noted for submission to God's will and for peace. Thus, the first three Choirs constitute the First hierarchy which is related to divine mysteries. The Second Hierarchy, the next three Choirs, deal with the management of human affairs as follows: Dominations display zeal for the maintenance of

God's authority. Virtues carry the message of the Dominations, and Powers fight against the evil spirits. The Third Hierarchy, the final three Choirs, have these duties: the Principalities announce divine things. They are responsible for the protection of our country and of the world. They help every soul to attain the degree of holiness to which God calls it. Father also said that each church has an Angel from this Choir assigned as its protector. The Archangels are entrusted with the more important missions of men: the Pope, the Bishops, etc. Finally, the Angels, the ninth Choir, are messengers sent to men. Guardian Angels and special assistants to us are in this Choir.

Whenever Father spoke of the Seraphim and tried to describe them, he would begin as though he were going to give a detailed account of their appearance. Immediately, however, as he spoke, it became obvious that he must have seen Seraphs. He was hardly able to describe their beauty, except to say that they were pure flame, burning with love for God. From subsequent conversations I became convinced that he had them in his presence.

I learned too, that every home has an Angel assigned to guard it. Father said that we should have special devotion to the Angels (all nine Choirs), and that the Archangels, as we call Saint Michael, Saint Gabriel and Saint Raphael, may actually be Seraphim. He said that he knew someone who had St. Michael for an Angel. He explained in his talks that the word "Angel" as we use it, applies to all members of the nine Choirs and also happens to be the specific name of the ninth Choir. In like manner, we sometimes use the word "Archangel" to mean someone higher than an Angel, and it also is the specific name of the eighth Choir.

Father said that St. Vincent Ferrer is the sixth Angel of the Apocalypse. He also emphasized the devotion which St. Anthony Claret had for the angels and cited the occasions on which the saint was visibly assisted by them. In further discussion we learned that Our Lord had revealed to St. Anthony Claret that He had made him the seventh Angel of the Apocalypse. This latter fact was also published several years later by Father Aloysius in an article entitled: "Seventh Angel of the Apocalypse" which he wrote for the January-February 1971 issue of Soul Magazine.

EXTRAORDINARY EVENTS

The trips from La Verne to Los Angeles, made for many weeks, were beset by mechanical difficulties with our car. Seldom could we use the freeways for fear of breakdowns. Ultimately, I got wise and asked Father to bless our car. It was then that travel became much easier. When he gave us this blessing, he also blessed our children with Holy Water, and they thoroughly enjoyed it. At the age of three, Dan thought that this was wonderful. He and the rest of the children had such a beautiful love for Father that they would fall to their knees whenever he approached. It would be impossible for Marion and me to visit privately with Father had the children not been provided for. Here also, was the hand of God upon us, for He had sent Joan Davis, a recent graduate from Mission High School in San Gabriel, to be our "daughter." Joan had been our babysitter at the Los Angeles Orphanage whenever we went there to visit Sister Henrietta (my sister Gertrude); so she had become part of the family. At the time that Joan came to live with us, we didn't know how necessary her help would be during the painful journey that was to ensue.

In February 1961, Marion and I decided to become daily communicants during Lent, which was soon to begin. Marion, however, suggested that we not wait for Lent, but rather that we begin immediately on February 12th. Thus we began daily Communion and continued to follow this practice throughout Lent and beyond. When Marion became too ill to attend Mass, I would ask one of our parish priests to bring Holy Communion to her at home. At times, I felt that this request was too much of an imposition on our priests; therefore, I resorted to asking them frequently, rather than daily. Fortunately, however, I myself was able to continue to receive uninterruptedly.

On Sundays, we went to the Claretian House at about 12:30 for the 2 P.M. novena. There were a few seats on the veranda, which hardly accommodated the line that formed, waiting for the doors to open. We knew that space within the chapel was at a premium, and it was only by an early arrival that one could be assured of getting inside. When all of the seats on the veranda were occupied then those who arrived later would stand in line. We usually scheduled our trip in time for Marion to get a seat because she was quite ill, and for her to stand for any period of time was very tiring. One Sunday, while she was seated, waiting for the doors to open, she noticed that a woman, whom she deemed to be sicker than herself, happened to be standing. Feeling compassion, Marion gave her seat and position in line to her. Subsequently, when we went inside, we were in a poor location and in the middle of a crowd near the chapel doorway. When Father Aloysius had completed the novena prayers and was ready to impart his individual blessing on the congregation, he suddenly walked through the crowd and went to Marion to bless her first. It was as though he had seen the sacrifice that she had made and didn't want her to wait any longer.

Many sick people attended these novenas. Numerous physical and mental problems existed in our midst. Some of these people would be cured, but all, if they were in proper disposition, received miracles of grace. In his talks to the people, Father often informed the crowd of miraculous healings that Almighty God had effected in the preceding week.

First Friday was always a special day at the Provincial House. Several Claretian Guilds met during the month at Holy Mass, but I believe that the First Friday meeting was the most populous one. Before the new house was built, it was necessary to use the chapel at the rear of the grounds, adjacent to the tennis courts. The additional space in this location, although not adequate, could better accommodate the crowd, and the rustic decor provided a peaceful setting.

Frequently, Father asked me to serve his Mass on First Friday. To attend the Holy Sacrifice is surely our greatest privilege. Additionally, it is a special honor to be invited to serve. On one of these Fridays, after Father had finished the Mass and was about to begin Benediction, he ascended the altar, and then motioned back to me to indicate that he didn't have a monstrance. Right away, I left the altar and went into the sacristy. As I was walking, however, I felt within myself that the trip was futile; I clearly recalled that before Mass one of the Claretians had closed the doors to the cabinet that housed the sacred vessels. I had definitely seen him lock these doors before he left, heading for the main house. Nevertheless, I knew that I should at least try to open the cabinet to get the monstrance, because there was the possibility that he didn't do a good job in locking it. After all, Father was waiting at this time on the altar to begin Benediction, and he needed that monstrance. How correct I was in my anticipation; my efforts to open the doors were fruitless. They were really locked! Disappointed and helpless, I went to the entrance of the sacristy, where I could see Brother Salvatore Azzarello at the organ. My motions caught his attention. He stopped playing and came past the altar into the sacristy to see what I wanted. When Brother heard my plight, he walked over to the cabinet and without a key, opened the door with ease. There could be no doubt then, that Our Lord wanted us to have Benediction that day.

During the same time frame, perhaps a few weeks later, another event relating to Benediction occurred. Father had exposed the Blessed Sacrament and was now kneeling at the foot of the altar reciting numerous prayers. I knelt by his side with the smoking thurible close at hand. It seemed to smoke excessively during these long prayers, and it was certainly getting hot. Then came the time for Father to offer incense. We both stood as I gave him the incense boat and kept the thurible. When I held it, I was surprised to see that is was not the conventional censer with which I was familiar. It did not have the usual two-chain system, one for support and one for operating the lid. Instead, this unit had a single chain which was attached to the base; in order to place incense on the burning coal, you would have to grasp the top of the chamber with your hand as the only means of opening it. I remembered that it had been smoking a lot, and by now the top could be very hot -- but then again, maybe it wouldn't be too bad. I held the base of the thurible in my left hand while using my right hand to grab the top. It was exceedingly hot! I had no choice but to drop the lid immediately. Father was standing there waiting -- incense boat in hand. The congregation was waiting, and most importantly, the Blessed Sacrament was waiting. There I stood, with two fingers on my right hand smarting terribly from the momentary contact with the hot lid of the censor. Promptly, I said a silent prayer before the Holy Eucharist: "Lord, I have two more fingers on my left hand; I'll give those to you, and then that's all I have." By changing hands, so that the base of the unit was now in my right hand, my left was free for a second attempt at the lid. Quickly, I grasped the menacing cover. I was able to hold it and lift it open with absolute comfort! Slowly and methodically, Father spooned the beads of incense over the glowing coals. Astonished, I realized that my left hand was immune to the severe heat. All this time, my right hand burned intensely. Later, in the sacristy, when services were over, Father said: "You burned your hand," as he grasped it with his own and rubbed my painful fingers. Immediately, the pain began to subside until it was quickly gone. I turned to Father and asked: "Why is it that these fingers on my right hand burn so badly after holding the top just for an instant, whereas, my left hand, which held the lid for so long, has no pain whatsoever?" Father's reply was: "God wants to show you how much He loves you. "

There was a time when Father heard confessions on Thursdays at the San Gabriel Mission. On one such Thursday, June 1, 1961, Marion and I arrived at the Provincial House at about four o'clock. This was an unusually late time for us to visit with Father. When we did see him, he blessed us and apologized for not having more time to talk. He was in a hurry, because it was now about 4:35, and he was due to leave for San Gabriel. When Father left the room and I had the opportunity to talk to his driver, Brother Larry, I asked him if he knew how bad the traffic would be at five o'clock, passing through Los Angeles on the way to San Gabriel. Oh yes, he was quite familiar with it, because he drove Father that way every week at this time, but he surely didn't observe any traffic. Repeatedly, he stated that he never noticed any traffic. That, I couldn't understand, because everybody knows the traffic congestion in the heart of Los Angeles at five o'clock. In a few minutes, Marion and I drove off and took the route homeward right through downtown Los Angeles. As expected, traffic was following its usual heavy pattern. When we stopped for a signal light on Main Street, there on our left was the Claretian car with Brother Larry and Father Aloysius. Father motioned to me to follow him, which I did. We then proceeded to drive all the way to San Gabriel as Brother Larry had predicted, without a traffic problem. It was necessary for us to stop only once during that trip: a journey of about fifteen miles.

When we reached San Gabriel, Marion wasn't feeling well. I got out of the car alone and went over to Father's car. He was delighted that we had come, and now he felt that he had the time to spend a few moments with me. I hadn't told him previously, but I needed to talk to him that day. How disappointed I was at the Claretian House when he told me that he wouldn't have time to visit. Now, in San Gabriel, the time was being given to me. God, of course, knew my needs and provided. I spoke to Father about the particular matter that concerned me. I was very thankful indeed for this opportunity. After that, Father and I walked through the garden. We went to the section that had been made into a small Claretian cemetery. It was here now that Father told me he too wished to be buried. Providentially, his wish was granted. Twenty years later, he was laid to rest in this beautiful garden and Our Gracious Lord ordained that I would have the privilege of serving as one of his pallbearers.

One afternoon, we had a visit scheduled with Marion's physician, Dr. Lawrence Crowley. We had arranged also to squeeze in some time with Fr. Aloysius in the latter part of the morning. When we met Father, it was apparent that he was quite busy and didn't have his usual tranquility. After a brief chat, he blessed us and sadly announced that he had to leave. We tried to ease his chagrin, caused by the limited time that was available and mentioned that we must leave anyway for our doctor's appointment. At that, Father responded: "The doctor will say that you are better." Shortly thereafter, we left and proceeded to the doctor's office in Pomona. After checking in at the desk, we took seats in the waiting room with numerous other patients. Scarcely did I have time to pick up a magazine, when the door opened and the doctor come into the waiting room. He strode over to Marion, addressing her as follows: "Well, you're better." After this terse statement, without uttering another word, he dashed back into his office. In amazement, I sat there pondering the fact that this man, whom Father had never met, had just spoken the phrase which had been foretold to me.

Because of the great discomfort that Marion experienced with her illness, it was often difficult for her to sleep. In order for me to get adequate rest before going to work, I frequently slept in another room. About four o'clock one morning, I was startled by an overpowering sensation that I was not alone; rather, Father was there with me, putting me at peace. When I had the opportunity, I questioned him as to whether he had bilocated at that time. He answered with his usual downward glance and smile, saying that he was not aware of it, but that other people had also told him of similar experiences.

In La Verne a towering ash tree gives mute testimony to the efficacy of a blessing by this holy priest. Our son, Steve, brought home a very small tree one day from school, a typical project for a youngster. We planted the tree in our backyard, but it didn't fare too well. That is, it didn't do well until Father blessed it on one of his visits. Thereafter, this tree flourished; the massive trunk always reminded us of its benefactor.

Father Aloysius was most diligent in his prayers, yet, he strove to reach greater heights. When I told him that St. Anthony Claret prayed very much, he took it as providential that he too must pray more.

Marion's education had been provided by the public school system in New Orleans. Thus, she was not privileged as I was to have formal Catholic training. At opportune moments we discussed various aspects of our faith upon which I could elaborate. I remembered one case where these discussions prompted me to make up a story to illustrate a point pertinent to our topic. In the days which followed, I heard this **very story** repeated to us by Father Aloysius as a means of explaining **his** thoughts.

It is important to mention that whenever Father was granted an answer to his prayers, whereby a miracle or gift on any kind was received, he forcefully made it known, time and time again, that he himself had done nothing! Everything came from the Almighty God. Rarely did he use the word "God" by itself. He always preferred to say

"Almighty God." His prayerfulness knew no bounds. He was not one for idle chatter, but he enthusiastically engaged in meaningful conversations and imparted earnest priestly blessings whenever the opportunity presented itself. Father often told us that every blessing provided grace. He went on further to say that sometimes physical healing occurred, but always, with proper disposition, spiritual healing was received.

In an effort to stop the spread of her cancer, Marion received radiation treatments. Her physical condition was very poor due to the deteriorated condition of her spine and the weakness brought on by radiation. It was at this time, and under these conditions in early 1961, that we made frequent daytime visits to the Provincial House to receive Father's blessing and spiritual counsel. On some of these trips Marion had to lie on the back seat of the car because she felt so badly. Then, upon arrival at the Claretian House, she required considerable help to negotiate the front steps. In the parlor, Father would bless her, and he would unfailingly follow up with the entreaty: "Now, walk down those steps." The steps referred to at this time were those at the back of the house, which were equally as steep as the ones in the front. Yet she traversed them with ease. She did not walk, she ran, up and down, over and over again, with no difficulty whatsoever. Fearful that she might hurt herself, I was always the one to bring this exercise to a close. Upon leaving the Provincial House, however, it was a different story. Marion would again return to her former condition of helplessness. At home she required assistance to go from her bed to the bathroom; a series of chairs would provide the necessary support. One day, our five year old redhead, Gail, saw her struggle. She stood firmly by the bed with her back toward her mother and said:

"Mommy, you can lean on me." In the years that followed, I frequently reminded Gail of the tender love that she had given to her mother. She had not failed to notice the devotion often displayed by her nine year old sister, Linda.

Marion had numbness creep up her arm, then envelop her tongue, and her nose would lose sensation. At these times, I didn't know what was coming next; I was devastated! Through so many examples of divine intervention, I had thought that a miraculous cure would soon be forthcoming. Now I was faced with an obvious and serious reversal.

Our Spiritual Father was most generous with his time. On days that we did not see him, we would telephone. It was commonplace for him to bless us over the phone. We had an efficient communication system most of the time, but on many occasions when I called him, the system became incredibly poor. What persistent difficulty I encountered! During one of these conversations I told him I would pray for him to receive the same gift which many years before had been granted to Saint Anthony Mary Claret. The gift about which I spoke was the miraculous retention within himself of the Holy Eucharist. Father then responded in these words: "Francis, I already have it." Upon hearing these words, I was dumbfounded. In a subsequent conversation, I told him that this revelation gave me unparalleled inner peace which lasted for an entire day. I was deeply grateful and awe struck with such a disclosure. He said that this sacred privilege was given to him in Chicago, on Holy Thursday, in 1941. I now learned that he resembled St. Anthony Claret not only in prayer, but also in this indescribable grace. Never, when praying with us, did he exclude St. Anthony whose virtues he extolled.

Father also spoke to me of his earlier years in Chicago, where he knew a holy woman, a nun, I believe, who had the power to heal. She told him that one day he too would be given this power. On Holy Thursday, a community of sisters, perhaps including this nun, had been in the chapel with Father when he received the Eucharistic privilege. They had seen rays emanating from the tabernacle toward him as he received the gift of retention of the Sacred Species. This wonderful grace delighted me so much that I wanted to tell everybody about it. Father would not allow that, however. When I asked for permission to speak of this marvelous gift, in profound humility he would deny me. Finally, one day, I was able to get his approval to tell certain persons. After that, he reluctantly conceded to me in this matter. When in his company, the Divine Presence was most often sensed.

Father's keen insight into the lives of certain individuals was unusual. On one occasion, early in our acquaintance, I made a general confession during which he proceeded to speak for me, stating the necessary details which I had difficulty in supplying. He then asked if he had been correct. I assured him that he had.

On a smoggy day, while driving to Los Angeles, I had a problem with one of my eyes. I had already seen a doctor about it and applied the medicine, but smog brought about greater irritation. I really didn't think it looked as bad as it felt. I was surprised, during his discourse, when Father called attention to my pain and volunteered his blessing. The doctor had told me that this chalazion could be treated, but it was chronic. However, after his blessing, Father said that my eye would be well. And so it was. I no longer needed the medicine.

Father's ability to discern illness was displayed many times. It was also possible for Father to detect cancer by smell. He told me of this capability on a few occasions.

Whenever we would talk of the sicknesses and calamities which occur in life, Father was consistent and emphatic in his explanation that God **permits** these things to happen. When, perhaps, I might say in my discussion that God allows things to happen, Father would be quick to correct me, saying: "God permits it to happen." This word "permits" was very important to Father Aloysius.

It is consoling to recall Father's description of the role of the deceased. He said that our dear departed ones are separated from us as though by a veil. We should never think that we are forgotten or alone for they are closer to us in death than they were in life. How comforting this fact can be when we feel that we have lost someone forever.

On First Friday, whenever Marion could muster the strength, we would both attend Father's Mass. On June 2, 1961, First Friday, Marion was feeling particularly depressed. She used her last bit of energy to make the trip. Pretty soon, I realized that it would be a major problem for her to get to the altar at Communion time. Since I was serving the Mass, I was not readily available to assist her. This problem concerned me. I pondered how many other people attending this Mass were also seriously ill. Father was always surrounded by sick people. Once again, God used Father Aloysius to display His concern in our turmoil. At Communion time, without any hesitation, Father strode off the altar and worked his way through the crowd. He went directly to Marion and gave her Holy Communion.

The lives of Marion and Father were closely linked. During the early part of 1961, Marion grew progressively worse until about summertime. Needless to say, Father was praying incessantly for her. Then, strangely, Father became sick himself, and he gradually grew worse. Simultaneously, Marion gradually grew better. This situation continued until she had gone from death's door to apparently complete health. She was able to drive her car and function in her household, just as before. At this time, Father, however, was dying; x-rays showed a tumor in his head. Later, on many occasions he recounted this era of his life. He prayed to Our Blessed Mother that she would heal him and allow him therefore to continue helping people. As usual, he re-dedicated himself to her. He related that the Blessed Mother then placed her hand on his head, and he was instantly cured. Moments later, when they were preparing for surgery, the doctor looked at the latest x-rays of Father's head. When he saw that Father had been miraculously cured, he prostrated himself on the floor.

Now, both Father and Marion were well again. This respite, however, was short lived. On the day before the feast of the Immaculate Conception in December 1961, while at the Claretian House, Marion and I went into the garden. She sensed a recurrence of her malady. From then onward, her health faded. She spent most of the time in bed; she suffered acutely. Her headaches were torturous and the accompanying nausea was most discomforting. She now had cerebral metastasis. On the Feast of Our Lady of Lourdes, February 11, 1962, she fell into a coma and died early the next morning, exactly one year after we had become daily communicants. On each of the days prior to her death, I had been phoning Father. During these conversations, invariably, I reflected on how many days were remaining to complete one year of daily Communions. In effect, I was unknowingly giving a countdown to her death. Her painful journey had ended. I phoned Father Aloysius at 4:00 A.M. and again received his solace. He thought that Marion had gone straight to Heaven, but he would say Mass for her at 6:30 A.M. Thus, by virtue of the "heroic privilege" that he had, her soul would be released to Heaven, if it had gone to Purgatory. She died wearing her brown Scapular after giving a gallant example of conformance to God's Will and bearing the suffering which it entailed. Marion's spiritual state, molded by Father, can best be expressed by her own words on the last Christmas card she gave to me:

"Our Prayer--God's Will be done.
Holy Mother help us!"

DIVINE CONSOLATION

On Tuesday, February l3th, Father Aloysius came to our church, Holy Name of Mary, with Fr. Frank Ambrosi, C.M.F., and two Claretian Brothers to recite the Rosary. On February l4th, Father conducted the funeral and said Requiem High Mass with Fr. Ambrosi and Fr. Barron, also a Claretian. Father Ambrosi delivered the eulogy. Later, Father Aloysius told me that he, himself, wanted to speak but hesitated for fear that the people would think his homily was strange. He proceeded to give his sermon to me in private. Father said Marion's suffering was like the Sorrowful Mysteries of the Rosary. Her mental anguish upon learning of her disease was analogous to the first mystery, the Agony in the Garden. The second, her severe back aches were like the Scourging. The third, her

excruciating headaches resembled the Crowning with
Thorns. The fourth, she Carried her Cross. The fifth
mystery was her Death.

Father was our very dear friend. Not only was he
supportive during this arduous trial, but he remained my
Spiritual Father thereafter.

On certain occasions after Marion's death, I began to feel
the overwhelming power of God in a manner most difficult
to describe--totally peaceful, totally encompassed, a sense
of utmost satisfaction. Upon the first occurrence of these
events, I immediately sought out Father for an explanation.
He was very happy for me and said that what I had was the
"experiential presence" of God. I was humbled beyond
words. We often talked about these experiences because
Father would query me about their frequency. I remember
telling him that there never was any way to predict such an
event; it could be while I was at Mass or even when I was
completely engrossed in some non-spiritual endeavor. His
prayers and intercessions to Our Lady were the means by
which I obtained many graces.

Also in 1962, shortly after Marion's death, a priest at St.
Joseph's Church in Pomona, Father Jerome Cummings,
made a very strange statement to me in the confessional.
Here was a priest that I had never met, telling me
something that was seemingly impossible. As usual, I
raced to Father Aloysius and told him what the priest had
said. I knew that it would require an instant miracle for the
priest's strange prediction to be correct. When hearing of
this incident, Father Aloysius was greatly pleased and told
me that he had prayed that I would receive this grace.

Through his prayers I did immediately receive a miracle from God as the priest in the confessional had foretold.

Since I had six young children to raise, the oldest being twelve and the youngest two, I wanted to take special care of my health for their sake. During a routine physical examination, the doctor reported that I had ischemia of the left ventricle in my heart. Perhaps this was true, perhaps they had made an error. In any event, after receiving Father's blessing and returning to the doctor, a new electrocardiogram showed no problem whatsoever.

I recall one particular First Friday when we were having the usual guild meeting and breakfast in the garden. Father introduced me to a prominent screen actress, Maureen O'Hara and her family. It was a joyful reunion as they gathered around him in gratitude. The mother had just been released from the hospital, perfectly well. Father had blessed her and prayed that she be cured from terminal cancer when she had but a few days to live. During the second Joyful mystery, she was cured -- Father always had a special love for this decade of the Rosary: the Visitation. When this woman died about three months later, Father's explanation to my "why," was that God apparently wanted to give her more time.

During the year 1954, while in New Orleans before we moved to California, I had experienced a spontaneous pneumothorax, a sudden lung collapse. It was weeks before I was able to return to work and months before I felt right again. Thus, in these later years while in California when I experienced the same pain, I likened it to my previous ailment. I phoned Father and received his blessing. Again I was well. Of course, without a medical diagnosis, it is not certain that this "attack" was identical to the former condition, but whatever it was, it was gone.

A friend of Father's, Sister Lucy, was to make her profession in the Carmelite Order in Long Beach on April 27, 1962. I was privileged to drive Father there and witness the celebration. This event gave him great satisfaction as did all sacred ceremonies. I too was profoundly edified and thankful to have been asked to accompany him. It was on such trips as this, when Father and I were alone and didn't have the interruption of door bells and telephones that I profited from his counseling.

It was Father's delight to visit the Los Angeles County Fair in Pomona whenever possible. At times I felt guilty offering Father such a trip when he appeared too tired; yet, I knew that he wanted me to do so. I would drive him there, and he would particularly enjoy the flower and garden displays. He continually found new strength in his admiration for God's creation. At times like this, his energy far exceeded mine.

One Sunday afternoon in 1962, while attending the novena at the Provincial House, I saw a friend of mine, Bob Mihalco. Until this time I had not realized that he was a Catholic. After the novena, he and his wife, Rolande, received Fr. Aloysius' blessing because she had melanoma. It was not long after this meeting that we became good friends, and I visited the Mihalcos frequently. In their effort to gain a further understanding of their faith, they posed many questions to me. I was happy to aid them in any way possible, and though I answered their inquiries, I felt fearful that I might not be answering their questions well enough and unknowingly lead them into error. I doubted my capability and was fearful of the responsibility of guiding these concerned souls at a time of such great distress. I expressed my uneasiness to Fr. Aloysius, and he responded: "Go visit them as often as possible, and don't worry about your answers to their questions. I will send my Guardian Angel with you." Thereafter, regardless of the difficulties in my schedule, I found time to drive from La Verne to Ontario frequently. Many times I took my son, Dan, with me so that he could visit with Bob's young son, Kurt. Thankful to have the assistance of Father's Guardian Angel, I proceeded to accept and answer all inquiries, and we had many pleasant spiritual visits. Bob and I would even see each other sometimes during the day, since we both worked at the same company. I would often repeat to him the worn out phrase: "Let me know if there is something that I can do for you." We wonder if such a statement will ever elicit a response. In this case, the day came that brought a response. On September 6, 1962, Bob called me to say that Rolande was dying, and could I please bring Fr. Aloysius to her. Surely I couldn't promise to do so, because I didn't know Father's availability, but I told Bob that I would do my best. Then, by a brief phone call I was quickly assured that he would be glad to visit Rolande, but he had no transportation. Fortunately I was able to get off of work. I picked up Father, and we began our fifty mile drive to Ontario. Aside from Father's greeting to me, he hardly said another word; but we prayed, and we prayed. Before the day was over, Father had recited thirty-five decades of the Rosary during our travels.

When we arrived at the Mihalco residence, Bob took us to Rolande, who lay in bed with a gaunt expression on her face. It was obvious that she was in a coma. Father prayed over her and blessed her, but she remained motionless, her mouth open, and her eyes in a blank stare. Father then decided to give Rolande a special blessing for the dying, so that she might receive a plenary indulgence. During this blessing, she briefly changed her expression, apparently indicating acknowledgement of the indulgence. She then lapsed back into her previous state. After many prayers and words of comfort to Bob and to Rolande's sister, a nurse, who was there caring for her, Father left. While riding back to Los Angeles, he continued his prayers as before --- reverently, tirelessly and hopefully. Then I dropped Father off and proceeded back to my home in La Verne. When I arrived, I was told that Bob had phoned, and I should call him back immediately, which I did. He said that Rolande had died. I went to his house at once. Now, even though she was dead, Rolande appeared exactly as she had before: mouth open, gaunt face and blank stare. We knelt at the foot of her bed and again prayed the Holy Rosary. Then, leaving Rolande's sister, Alice, in the room, Bob and I went into the living room to await the undertaker who had already been called. While we sat there, Alice came in at least three times, urging us to come back into the bedroom to see Rolande. Each time we excitedly went with her, and each time we witnessed a progressive change in Rolande's countenance. Her mouth and eyes were closing, and her face was now becoming relaxed. Finally, when the time came to remove her body, I vividly recall sitting with Bob as she was rolled through the living room. There was a beautiful, peaceful smile on her face. It was obvious that Father's prayers had been heard.

Throughout his lifetime, the sanctity of Father Aloysius shone forth like a beacon. Many people searched him out; they constantly sought his blessing, his prayers and his advice. After his novena services, it was commonplace to see a table laden with religious articles awaiting his blessing. Father responded to this devotion with a total giving of himself. He met their needs with tender compassion. His paternal concern for the poor and the bereaved exemplified Christ Himself.

Father displayed an affection for many of the saints. His particular devotion for Saint Therese, The Little Flower, was evident when he gave me some beautiful rose petals which were in an envelope inscribed: "Roses blessed with the Carmelite Blessing of Saint Therese on her feast day, October 3, 1962, by Father Aloysius, C.M.F., who has the necessary special faculties granted by the Carmelite Provincial of the United States."

Father gave me several books. In each of these he wrote a few words of encouragement. Particularly, I recall the "Little Office of The Blessed Virgin Mary," published by the Newman Press, and "The Sanctifier," by Archbishop Martinez. An important work that Father recommended was: "The City of God," by Sister Mary of Agreda, published by the Ave Maria Institute. He had read the four volumes written by this holy nun and firmly advocated this private revelation. Father George J. Blatter, under the pen name of Fiscar Marison, provided this superb translation from the original authorized Spanish edition. In fact, Fr. Blatter himself, had given Father Aloysius a copy of his work many years ago. Because of the strong influence which Father's recommendations carried with me, I borrowed "The City of God" from Katherine Morrow and eagerly read all volumes. After completing the series, I was especially impressed by the section within volume four, the Coronation, (page 297 to page 331) which deals with the experiences of St. James during his apostolate to Spain. The difficulties which this saint encountered prompted him to beseech the aid of Our Blessed Lady who was still alive. In response to his prayers, she was transported by the Angels to Granada where he was imprisoned. She also went to him in Saragossa. There she left her own likeness, carved by the Angels, placed atop a marble or jasper column, which at her command was to be housed within a church to be built in her name. She promised that abundant graces from Almighty God would be granted here through her intercession, provided that we ask in sincere piety and with true faith. At once, Saragossa rose to special significance in my life. I longed for the day when I could visit there to pray for the signal intercession of Our Holy Mother.

In early 1963, Father was sent to Spain; it was a sad day indeed when he left. Before going, he gave me a delightfully sweet statue of St. Joseph with the Child Jesus at about eight years of age, standing on His toes, reaching up to His father. St. Joseph, in turn, is bent at the waist, so that he can cup the Child's head in his hands. This statue is my most prized possession.

Father was gone now, and I had lost my source of guidance. Once, however, when I felt that I needed his help, I did not hesitate to telephone him in Bilbao, Spain. He and I had previously discussed the situation at issue, and he had told me that when he went to Saragossa, he would ask the Blessed Mother my question. Due to the great difference in time, my telephone connection with Father was not completed until about one o'clock in the morning, California time. I was elated to hear Father's voice; until now, our only communication had been by mail. He explained to me why my call had been completed at that precise time. He had just returned from Saragossa and felt that he had an answer to my prayer. Eagerly I listened, for Father's voice was coming through very well. Then, all of a sudden, when he began to tell me what the Blessed Mother had said, I could no longer understand him, for his voice was drowned out by a violent rattling of the doorknob in my bedroom. After several seconds, the rattling ceased, but Father had finished giving his message. I told him that I couldn't understand what he said and asked him to repeat it. Graciously, he did so, but again I was victimized by the rattling of my doorknob. How could this be? I knew my children were asleep. After waiting for the noise to stop, I asked Father again to repeat his message. He said that the devil didn't want me to hear it; so he repeated it again, and this time his words were quite discernible. By a subsequent search of the house, I ascertained that all of the children were, in fact, asleep.

On July 27, 1963, when in Bilbao, Father wrote a most touching letter:

"*********If God wants me to be isolated from my friends in America, may His Holy Will be most welcome. It is a great consolation for me to pray for your intentions, but particularly for your own self, dear Francis. May I beg of you most humbly to pray that I be always identified with the Holy Will of God without counting the cost. You are a tremendous friend to me and I need your prayer and your sacrifice in the future as much or more than in the past. I will pay you back with all that I am and with all that I have before the throne of the Almighty God.

Most gratefully in the I. Heart of Mary Fr. Aloysius Ellacuria, C.M.F.

After these events, I longed more than ever to go to Saragossa. Some years later, when Father had returned to the states, and he was arranging to lead a pilgrimage to European shrines, including Saragossa, I prayed to be able to go with him. Such a trip, however, was impossible, because my children were too young for me to leave them. Many people accompanied Father, including Katherine Morrow and Mary Naughten. Several months later, I met Mary through Katherine Morrow and the prayers of Fr. Aloysius.

Later in 1963, Father returned from Spain and then when he was in Phoenix, I took my family there several times to see him. We went by automobile, bus and plane: whatever was necessary at the time. On the first visit, he was in the hospital, and when I went to his room, he reached down and pulled out a relic of St. Anthony Claret to give me. Did he know that I had prayed for this?

We also visited Father when he was the pastor at Immaculate Heart Of Mary Church in Phoenix. His mind was occupied with the events surrounding a wedding that he had performed just a few days earlier. He had prayed ardently for the young couple during the ceremony and long after it. Father recalled how the new bride had selected a single white rose to be dedicated to the Blessed Mother. It was placed beneath the picture of Our Lady which adorned the wall just above the votive candles. It was summertime now in Phoenix, about three days later. The temperature was 109 degrees, and right above the candles where the rose was situated it must have been 130 degrees or so. Yet, this rose was fresh as ever: it had not lost any of its texture. When I walked with Father through the church, we paused with a smile as we looked up at the rose. It was certainly unusual for a rose to behave this way, but I had become accustomed to the unusual. The next day when I was preparing to leave Phoenix, Father shared with me his new found data. Upon close examination he found out that the beautiful white rose was a beautiful white artificial rose. For sure, Father was only human.

Even San Antonio wasn't too far to drive either; so we went to see Father when he was there also. Wherever Father was stationed, he reflected in his actions the piety and humility that were his hallmark. All assignments were accepted with holy obedience.

Even muscles bruised in Little League baseball responded to Father's plea. I remember our son, Steve, confidently placing his sore leg in Father's care. A much more serious leg ailment also was cured when Steve Damico met Father and sought relief for his long standing feverish illness. Cellulitis infection in his leg would produce a 105 degree temperature. Subsequently, although he sustains minor inconvenience, he has had no major problem with his leg. He is able to participate in sporting events, and the fever no longer exists.

When Mary Naughten and I were contemplating marriage in 1969, we visited Father Aloysius. While driving to Los Angeles for this visit, we began discussing a certain scriptural passage. It was not a lengthy discussion, for it took only a few minutes. Upon our arrival, Father greeted us cordially and counseled us for a half hour or so. Then he blessed us, and we prepared to leave. We had gone out the front door, closed it and were walking away, when Father opened the door just slightly, enough to put his head through, and made a few comments on the identical biblical passage that Mary and I had previously discussed in private. Without a further word, but with a big smile, Father closed the door again and disappeared. In our talk, Father had advised us to get married. Surely with his final message on departure, we were convinced that we should do so.

In Mary, I had been blessed with a helpmate to raise the children. She had known Father Aloysius independently and had grown spiritually through attendance at his devotions.

After our marriage, on September 24, 1969, we lived in La Verne. Then, in March of 1973, we moved to Alta Loma. Father visited us many times at our home. He was able to relax and take siestas in our peaceful environs.

Sister Mary Joseph Bialgues, a member of the Order called: "The Little Sisters of Christ The King," came to the United States from France in January 1970, through the courtesy of Rita and Mary Ellen Benziger. Father Aloysius was informed of her forthcoming visit, and on December 6, 1969, in preparation for this event, he solicited the aid of Charles Carpenter as an interpreter. This holy nun had an extraordinary gift of grace, the gift of counsel. On many occasions she used this gift for the benefit of those who sought her guidance. It seemed perfectly natural that Father Aloysius should be involved with a nun who was so gifted. At Father's invitation, Mary and I met Sister Bialgues at the Benziger home. It was a fruitful spiritual experience to spend an afternoon with these two gifted mystics.

Sister Bialgues remained in this country about five weeks before returning to France early in February of 1970. on March 8, 1976, she died in her native country. Sister had come from a very large family, and during the Second World War, she, along with her brothers and sisters did whatever they could to aid the French Resistance. One of her brothers was frequently subjected to search by the Germans, and her family often was in hiding. At one time, Sister herself was taken prisoner by the Germans to a tower in Amiens. She was placed in a dungeon within the tower. Deprivation from food and drink in these confines had exacted a severe toll on her health. Yet, in spite of this handicap, she was to continue her life of devoted service for many years to come and provide spiritual sustenance to those who needed her.

In 1976, Father led another pilgrimage to Europe, and again he would include Saragossa in the itinerary. I hoped to make this trip and prepared by getting my passport. As the time grew closer, I felt once more that I should remain at home with my family. Here went my last opportunity to visit Saragossa with Father Aloysius. How many times had I prayed that I would make such a trip.

In October of 1979, my time arrived to make a pilgrimage to Europe! In order to make certain that I wouldn't miss Saragossa, I scheduled that shrine to be the first of our stops. Thus, on the feast of the Holy Rosary, my wife, Mary, and I departed for Spain. The day that we arrived in Saragossa, I was 54 years, 3 months and 28 days old. Remarkably, my age had almost coincided with the age of Our Lady when she had visited St. James in Saragossa.

The City of God (page 331 of the Coronation) states that she was 54 years, 3 months and 24 days old at that time.

The faithful from all stations in life were ministered to by Father Aloysius. He gave his time wherever it was needed. No sickness was hopeless, nor was any ailment too minor to gain heartfelt concern. An illustration of this concern was displayed for our daughter, Ann. It was after dark on a rainy Christmas night, in 1977, that he came up our driveway for what was to be his last visit to our home. Ann had gone to see him a couple of months earlier, and he wanted to remind her that he was praying for her intentions.

Father was always eager to see whoever needed him. Ben, my neighbor, was a case in point. I didn't know he was my neighbor until he got sick. When his absence in the community became apparent, it was brought to my attention. I visited Ben, learned that he was critically ill and was a fallen away Catholic. Thinking that perhaps he would like to return to his faith, I broached the subject. It didn't take long to find out that Ben didn't even want to talk about his faith.

Our visits were friendly as long as our discussions were limited to National Geographic, Reader's Digest, outdoor life and nature in general. Although he was confined to bed, his mind roamed through God's creation.

At one time, he was agreeable to a brief visit by our local priest and at a later date accepted a short visit by Father Aloysius. Even now, Ben still wasn't ready. Father prayed for him during the following weeks. Along with the many other intentions that were constantly put forth to him, he now had Ben in his daily prayers. Soon Ben went to the hospital and soon too, he became agreeable to prayer. On succeeding days, with each recital of the Hail Mary, he grew more peaceful. Now through Father's prayerful intercession, Ben was able to turn to God. It was no longer difficult for him to accept his faith and put it into practice. Ben then died in peace.

Mary and I continued to attend the Third Saturday Guild Mass and avail ourselves of the opportunity of seeing Father. When he became too ill to come to our home, we were most fortunate to be able to continue visiting with him at various locations. We made frequent trips to the Hollywood Presbyterian Medical Center where at one time he was convalescing. We also saw him at the St. John of God Nursing Home in Los Angeles and made one trip to the Carmel Residence at Fallbrook where the Carmelite Sisters cared for him. Our last hospital visit was a very brief meeting with Father at St. John's in Santa Monica. Father's illnesses now became more frequent and of longer duration.

ETERNAL REWARD

Early in 1981, Father's recurring heart problem brought about a steadily diminishing physical capability. It was consoling to know that Kevin Manion, a very dear friend of his, was ever present to help him. In March, I took Mary and her father, Malachy Naughten, to the Claretian House. When we saw Father, he had just left the chapel and was walking with difficulty down the hallway. He immediately reached out and blessed us. He expressed his compassion to Malachy who had recently lost his dear wife, Mary.

On April 6, 1981, Father Aloysius died. Mass of the Resurrection was concelebrated on Thursday April 9, at 7:30 P.M. at the San Gabriel Mission. Bishop Juan Arzube was the principal celebrant -- fondly, Father had cradled the Bishop's head in his arms when we gathered to celebrate Father's 50th Anniversary to the priesthood in 1979. Now, before beginning the Holy Sacrifice, Bishop Arzube stopped in procession before the altar and announced that Father had been close to us in life, and he remains close in death. "He has already answered my question," the Bishop said. He had asked what it was like to be in Heaven. Father told him that whatever we have to endure here on earth amounts to nothing in comparison to the treasure that God has in store for us. With that, the Bishop continued up the steps and began Mass. The church was full. I estimated 1300 people to be in attendance. I was later told that there were approximately 300 additional people outside who could not fit into the church. Father William King, the Claretian Superior, who had been so kind through the years, allowing me to see Father Aloysius frequently, had invited me to serve as a pallbearer.

On Friday, April l0th, after the 10:00 A.M. Rosary, Father was buried as he has wished, in the San Gabriel Mission grounds, where he had walked with me and where I now helped to bear his body.

No single individual impacted my life as did Father Aloysius. His spiritual guidance will remain with me forever. Even after his death, I am not abandoned. In July 1976, I began to experience a new series of physical setbacks. For five years I underwent every test that the doctors prescribed - all to no avail. My prayers seemed to provide no relief. Then, in 1981, my illness left me completely when Father Aloysius went to his eternal reward.

Now we all have a powerful intercessor who stands in Perpetual Adoration before the throne of God. He will remember each of us and will look with particular fatherly care upon the fledglings of his own formation: MISIONEROS DE ADORACION PERPETUA.

In Fatima, Portugal, on February 9, 1972, Father Aloysius founded the Missionaries of Perpetual Adoration of the Most Blessed Sacrament and Perpetual Veneration of the Immaculate Heart of Mary. This group strives to emulate the heroic life of its founder and put into their daily practice his constant diligence to prayer.

At his desk in Phoenix

PERSONAL DATA

Fr. John Aloysius Ellacuria Echevarria, CMF

Born on June 21, 1905, in the town of Yurre, Province of Vizcaya, Spain.

Father and Mother were Raymond and Martha.

Baptized on June 22, 1905, in Yurre in the parish of Our Lady of the Assumption by Fr. Mariano Echevarria.

First Holy Communion was on February 2, 1912, at Our Lady of the Assumption from the hands of the pastor, Fr. Hilario de Soloeta.

Confirmed in 1913 in Assumption parish by Bishop Cadena y Eleta, Titular of Vitoria, Alba, Spain.

Family home was in a suburb of Yurre called Caserio-Orue Barrio de San Cristobal, Yurre, Vizcaya, Spain. Raymond Ellacuria's occupation was that of a proprietor of farms, mountains and pastures and woody groves in and around Yurre.

Entered the Congregation on July 29, 1916, in the minor Seminary in Valmaseda, Vizcaya, Spain under the Perfect John Anthony Uriarte and Superior Jose Calvo.

Reception of the Holy Habit of the Congregation was on August 14, 1920, from the hands of Most Rev. Father Martin Alsina, CMF, Superior General.

Aloysius

Priestly Ordination was on November 3, 1929, in the city of Burgos by the Archbishop Dr. Emmanuel De Castro.

Chapter Twenty-Five

<u>Saintly Virtues:</u>

Four virtues play a pivotal role and accordingly are called "cardinal"; all the others are grouped around them. They are: prudence, justice, fortitude, and temperance. (CCC 1805)

The human virtues are rooted in the theological virtues, which adapt man's faculties for participation in the divine nature: for the theological virtues relate directly to God. They dispose Christians to live in a relationship with the Holy Trinity. They have the One and Triune God for their origin, motive, and object. (CCC 1812)

The theological virtues are the foundation of Christian moral activity; they animate it and give it its special character. They inform and give life to all the moral virtues. They are infused by God into the souls of the faithful to make them capable of acting as His children and of meriting eternal life. They are the pledge of the presence and action of the Holy Spirit in the faculties of the human being. (CCC 1813)

It is essential that we understand these theological virtues of Faith, Hope, and Charity in their origin, in their nature and of their ultimate fulfillment. When we study these characteristics and seek to find their implementation, it doesn't take long for us to find it in the life and actions of Father Aloysius.

The presence of God, the activity of God and the outpouring of Divine Love which emanated from Father Aloysius were so very obvious. They were exhibited by prayerful contact which he established between his spiritual children and God. By his counsel he taught us to see God in all things and to do all things for Him. Along with these actions, we were then to put our complete trust in Him who could not disappoint. Very necessary however was it for us to understand that our primary intention was always that God's Will be done. With this intent firmly implanted, it became easy to accept the answer to our prayer when that answer was not exactly what we asked for. The outcome of this acceptance of God's Holy Will was the gift of peace which prevailed oftentimes in the midst of trial. We became able to recognize the fact that our prayers are always heard and answered.

Most sweet and gentle kindness was the introduction used by Father Aloysius in his greeting to all. When illness or inner turmoil of visitors was then evident, the completion of this beautiful act of Love by Father was then his profound recourse to prayer and his actual sharing of the suffering. There could be no mistake in the fact that Father Aloysius would be completely overcome with compassion. Only Divine presence within him could make this deepest Love shine so brilliantly. When we show compassion, we imitate Father Aloysius who learned it from The Master.